# SOCIAL SERVICES: WHAT HAPPENS TO THE CLIENTS?

MARGO KOSS
HARRY HATRY
ANNIE MILLAR
THERESE VAN HOUTEN
*The Urban Institute*

KATHRYN CRADDOCK
WILLIAM BRIGHT
*Bureau of Social Services,
Chesapeake, Virginia*

GAYLE BURLESON
*Department of Human Resources
State of North Carolina*

JOYCE REARDON
*Department of Social Services
Durham County, North Carolina*

**THE URBAN INSTITUTE**

The research forming the basis for this publication has been supported by the U.S. Department of Health, Education, and Welfare, and the National Center for Productivity and Quality of Working Life. In addition, the city of Chesapeake, Virginia, the state of North Carolina, and the North Carolina counties of Stanly and Durham have been active participants in this work. The U.S. Office of Personnel Management provided contract administration for the last phase of the work.

The interpretations or conclusions are those of the authors and should not be attributed to these other agencies, or to The Urban Institute, its trustees, or to other organizations that support its research.

ISBN 87766-272-X

UI 1185-4


PLEASE REFER TO URI 28400 WHEN ORDERING

Available from:

Publications Office
The Urban Institute
2100 M Street, N.W.
Washington, D.C.  20037

List price:  $6.50

A/79/3M

# PREFACE

This report presents a set of procedures and the results of its testing by two local social service agencies. These procedures can be used by social service agencies to monitor changes in client functioning, well being, and client satisfaction after an agency's services have been provided to clients.

The current volume is the third of a series. The first two reported on the results of our examination of other outcome measurement efforts and our initial formulation of a questionnaire and procedures: Annie Millar, Harry Hatry, and Margo Koss, Monitoring the Outcomes of Social Services, Volume 1, Preliminary Suggestions, and Volume 2, A Review of Past Research and Test Activities (Washington, D.C.: The Urban Institute, May 1977). Since that effort, the questionnaire and many of the procedures have been pilot-tested with the Bureau of Social Services in Chesapeake, Virginia, the North Carolina Department of Human Resources, and the Department of Social Services in Durham County, North Carolina.

In light of the pilot test work, we have modified the initial questionnaire and procedures and offer here our recommendations together with the experience that led to them.

This outcome monitoring method is only one of several possible approaches to measuring outcomes, each of which has advantages and disadvantages. We do not attempt here to discuss the pros and cons of the different approaches; these were considered in Volumes 1 and 2. The current volume is offered as a guide to the one method that we tested. While further work should be done to refine and fully validate the method and to test its usefulness to social service agencies, the approach appears basically sound and well worth consideration by social service agencies.

# TABLE OF CONTENTS

## LIST OF EXHIBITS

# SUMMARY

## BACKGROUND AND OVERVIEW OF PROCEDURES

Information regarding the outcomes of services seems essential for good policy and program decisionmaking, but few social service agencies regularly monitor the outcomes of their services. While they collect data regarding service activity--numbers of clients served, numbers of casework interviews, and so on--agencies collect little systematic data on the outcomes of this activity. This major information gap exists in part because social service agencies lack practical procedures for large-scale monitoring of outcomes.

With the support of the U.S. Department of Health, Education, and Welfare, The Urban Institute undertook to develop practical outcome monitoring procedures for use by social service agencies.[1] After reviewing what had previously been done to develop outcome measures for social services, we focused on designing procedures based primarily on interviewing clients regarding their functioning and well-being and their satisfaction with services.

During the first phase of the effort, with the North Carolina Department of Human Resources, we identified a set of procedures for assessing outcomes and pretested a preliminary client outcome questionnaire. The results of this first year of work are contained a a two-volume report.[2]

During the second phase, pilot tests of the questionnaire and associated procedures were undertaken in two public social service agencies. The Chesapeake, Virginia, Bureau of Social Services tested the procedures, working directly with The Urban Institute. The North Carolina Department of Human Resources, with assistance from The Urban Institute, supervised testing in the Durham County Department of Social Services. These pilot tests led to numerous changes in the questionnaire and procedures.

---

1. The work focused on services and did not include income maintenance.

2. Annie Millar, Harry Hatry, and Margo Koss, Monitoring the Outcomes of Social Services, vols. 1 and 2 (Washington, D.C.: The Urban Institute, 1977). Volume 2 discusses previous work done by others in social services outcome measurement. Volume 1 contains preliminary suggestions for a method of client outcome measurement.

The outcome monitoring procedures include the following basic elements:

- Throughout the year (or in selected weeks or months), all clients (or a sample of clients) are interviewed near the time of application or at intake--"pre-service" interviews. These pre-service monitoring interviews are separate from routine intake casework interviews. Trained interviewers (who are not necessarily caseworkers) conduct the interviews either in person or by telephone. Interviewers use a structured questionnaire that includes questions about problems in a number of areas of functioning and well-being.

- Each client is interviewed again after some specified interval such as nine months--"follow-up" interviews. The questionnaires used at follow up are similar to those used at intake, except that they also include questions regarding client satisfaction with services and client perceptions of how their problems have changed and which services, if any, helped or hindered them.

- Information is obtained from client records regarding the type and amount of services provided to each client, plus some information on outcomes (such as placements), to supplement information collected in client interviews.

- Client pre-service, follow-up, and change "scores" are calculated and linked with information on services provided and on client characteristics to provide information to officials on outcomes for clients of various types, for different programs and facilities, and for different services.

## WHAT DATA ARE COLLECTED?   (CHAPTER 2, APPENDICES)

Exhibit 1 summarizes the specific data collected. Most data are obtained in client interviews. For each of several areas of client problems--physical health, mental distress, and so on--there is a group of questions in the client interview. Some limited data related to outcomes are also collected from records, to supplement client reports.

The procedures also provide for the collection of data on type of services received, number of caseworker-client contacts, and length of service for individual clients. We focused largely on developing outcome measures. We did not attempt to design comprehensive measures of service activity, but we would encourage agencies to add more refined and complete service measures. The usefulness of outcome monitoring data will be increased when the data link outcomes with detailed information about service activities.

Appendix 1 of this report presents an illustrative client interview questionnaire similar to those used in the pilot tests. Appendix 2 discusses the rationale for individual problem areas and questions. Appendices 3 and 4 present the results of our limited testing of the questionnaire's reliability and validity.

EXHIBIT 1:  DATA COLLECTED IN OUTCOME MONITORING

| Dimensions | Source of Data | | |
|---|---|---|---|
| | Pre-Service Client Interview | Follow-Up Client Interview | Agency Records or Case Records |
| 1. Physical Health | X | X | |
| 2. Performance of Activities of Daily Living | X | X | |
| 3. Physical Abuse | X | X | X |
| 4. Mental Distress | X | X | X |
| 5. Alcohol and Drug Abuse | X | X | X |
| 6. Family Strength | X | X | |
| 7. Quality of Substitute Care | X | X | X |
| 8. Child Problem Behavior and Parenting | X | X | |
| 9. Economic Self-Support and Security | X | X | |
| 10. Client Satisfaction and Perception of Change | | | |
|    Satisfaction with each specific service received | | X | |
|    Satisfaction with referrals to outside agencies for services not provided by public agency | | X | |
|    Promptness in obtaining services | | X | |
|    Ease of contacting workers | | X | |
|    Accessibility of agency offices | | X | |
|    Courtesy | | X | |
|    Overall satisfaction | | X | |
|    Client perception of change in each of the 9 problem areas (Physical Health, etc.) | | X | |
|    Overall perception of change | | X | |
| 11. Background Information | | | |
|    Age, sex, race, education, household composition, presenting problem | X | X[a] | |
| 12. Services Received | | | |
|    Services delivered to client between pre-service and follow-up interviews | | | X |
|    Number of caseworker contacts with client, telephone and in person | | X | X[b] |
|    Length of time during which client received services after pre-service interview | | | X |

a.  Age, sex, household composition, and the client's recollection of presenting problem are asked at follow up.  (Race and education are excluded at follow up since they are not likely to change.)  These questions provide a doublecheck that the same client is being interviewed.

b.  Information on number of contacts may or may not be available in agency records; if it is not, client reports will be the only source for these data.

This questionnaire is designed to be usable for most types of clients. Skip patterns and screening questions in the questionnaire are included to allow interviewers to skip inapplicable questions--such as child problem behavior questions for childless clients and questions on activities of daily living for clients without disabilities. In general, clients are interviewed at intake and follow up regarding all areas of functioning that are applicable, regardless of their "presenting problem" or the services they receive.

Several factors led us to choose this "whole client" design rather than provide procedures tailored to each particular service: (1) Often the presenting problem represents only one of several problems for which services are needed (in Chesapeake, clients reported an average of four major problems in the pre-service interviews). (2) Predicting what services any given client will receive is often impossible. (3) Predicting which aspects of functioning and well-being any given service will affect is also difficult. (4) Clients often receive more than one service (as did 46 percent of Chesapeake's pilot test clients) and are affected in several areas of functioning. For example, a client who receives child day care services might achieve economic self-support, feel better physically and emotionally, drink less alcohol, and the client's children's behavior might improve. Such a client might also receive counseling and job training. Rather than trying to guess what services a client will receive, and what aspects of a client's life will be affected by services, and then limiting data collection to those aspects, it seems preferable to monitor for a range of possible outcomes.

Although these procedures follow the general principle of examining outcomes for the "whole client," they provide data that can be used to study specific services. Data are obtained on the services each client received, and clients are asked about their satisfaction with each type of service. Outcome data can be grouped according to which services the clients received, and groups of questions that are particularly relevant for specific services can be singled out. For example, an agency studying outcomes for child day care clients might focus on child behavior, economic self-support, and family strength outcomes for all clients that received day care services during a certain period.

A number of components of the questionnaire are based on work done previously by others, but we found no single instrument that covered the range of outcomes required for comprehensive outcome monitoring. The questionnaire used in the pilot tests was new and untested. We pretested the questionnaire in two sites, made some reliability checks by reinterviewing some clients, interviewing their caseworkers, checking records for corroborative data, obtaining retrospective caseworker ratings of client functioning and change, and performing some statistical testing of the questionnaire.

The questionnaire appears to have reasonable "face validity" in the sense that it represents a consensus among a number of social workers and administrators as to what the important possible outcomes of social services are (a consensus that has held up with only minor differences among the agencies involved in the pilot tests). The question wording, some of which has been improved during the pilot tests, seems understandable to clients, and clients have been able and willing to respond. Client responses in initial interviews in the pretest were generally consistent with their responses upon reinterview and with caseworker reports. Caseworkers' retrospective before and after ratings of the pilot test clients were also largely consistent with client interview results, except that clients tended to report more problems than their caseworkers. The statistical studies of the questionnaire indicated good reliability. There were a few questions, however, that were difficult or sensitive for some clients--questions on family earnings, abuse, and drug and alcohol problems--and we have some concern about the reliability of these data. Further testing is indicated, and client reports in sensitive problem areas should be supplemented by information from records--for example, documented abuse, alcohol and drug problems.

Procedures for "scoring" (summarizing) each outcome dimension were developed and tested against the judgments of a small number of caseworkers regarding the severity of problems indicated by client responses on the questionnaire. While the scoring procedures held up well, they should be checked further and refined as experience with the data increases. In addition, further statistical testing of the questionnaire's reliability would be worthwhile. We think that the questionnaire can be improved and probably shortened somewhat if this further testing is done.

The procedures are not necessarily tied to the particular illustrative questionnaire presented in Appendix 1. Other questionnaires can be used with the procedures, or agencies can modify or expand this questionnaire to obtain more detail on outcomes of special interest.

## DATA-COLLECTION PROCEDURES (CHAPTER 3)

The interviewing procedures described in Chapter 3 appear workable. The length of the interviews (an average of about twenty-four minutes for pre-service interviews in Chesapeake and Durham, fifty minutes for follow-up interviews in Chesapeake, and forty-six minutes for follow-up interviews in Durham) did not cause significant problems; in the pilot tests over 99 percent of the interviews that were initiated were completed, with no indication of significant respondent fatigue.

Telephone interviews were successful and should be used wherever clients have convenient access to a telephone. Only those clients without access to telephones and those with special communication problems need to be interviewed by the more costly in-person procedure. The majority of the pilot test interviews were done by telephone (60 percent of 344) and the remainder were done in-person at the clients' homes (36 percent) or in-person at the agency offices (4 percent). A mail or other self-administered questionnaire was not tested; the length and content of the questionnaire and literacy problems of the client population would make self-administration by clients difficult. We do not rule out the possibility of self-administered questionnaires for some clients, however, provided that a shorter version of the questionnaire can be developed.

With careful selection, training, and supervision, nonprofessional trained interviewers can successfully administer the questionnaires. A small number of agency clerical staff and CETA workers were trained to administer the interviews in Chesapeake, and most of Durham's interviews were administered by outside interviewers.

The procedures require no regular participation by service caseworkers once the monitoring system is established. There are several reasons why we avoided using caseworkers to rate the condition of their own clients: (1) It is highly desirable to avoid requiring additional time and paperwork from already overburdened caseworkers. (2) It is difficult to obtain reliable, comparable ratings when many raters are involved. (3) Caseworkers usually are informed about clients' status only up to the termination of services, so that unless caseworkers made a special follow up (using scarce and costly professional time) there would be no way for caseworkers to judge to what extent client gains are maintained after termination. (4) Finally, having caseworkers provide outcome information on their own clients introduces a question of bias that can affect the credibility of the information for evaluation purposes. There is a potential conflict of interest if caseworkers' ratings are used to help evaluate the services they provide.

New service cases should be screened by an outcome monitoring coordinator, then assigned to trained interviewers who seek client consent and do the pre-service interviews. Before the interview, intake caseworkers or receptionists should give clients an information letter describing the study and informing them that an interviewer will contact them to see if they will participate and to interview them if they consent. Initially we tried a different procedure: Intake caseworkers obtained consents and referred clients to a coordinator. This procedure, however, took time out of the routine casework intake interviews. In addition, it required that a large number of caseworkers be trained in the administration of the informed consent procedures. Late in the Durham pilot test, the procedure was changed to that just suggested. Although this new procedure was tested only briefly, it appeared to work well.

We suggest that agencies implementing procedures such as these not incorporate written consents unless they are legally required to do so. In the tests, written consents were required from clients prior to interviewing them. This requirement caused considerable extra effort, since a number of clients who could otherwise have been interviewed by telephone had to be contacted in person. Since the procedures do not appear to pose any danger to clients, verbal consent seems sufficient provided that clients are fully informed and clearly advised that participation in the outcome interviewing is voluntary and that refusal will in no way affect the services they will receive.

Clients who complete pre-service interviews (or a subsample of these clients) should be interviewed again after a fixed interval of time, such as nine months. In order to capture how well clients continue to manage after services cease, we suggest that the follow-up interval be long enough to assure that a substantial percentage of the clients will no longer be receiving services.

Difficulty in locating clients for follow up was less of a problem than we had anticipated. Clients who had moved out of the local area or could not be found at follow up represented 7 percent of the total sample in both Chesapeake and Durham. (An additional 9 percent had been "lost" when they were not located by initial consent or the pre-service interview.) However, we tested

only one follow-up interval, seven to eight months, and therefore have no information regarding to what extent shorter intervals would improve location
rates or longer intervals degrade them. A parallel study that The Urban Institute is conducting on mental health client outcomes, however, found that
the number of "nonlocates" did not vary substantially between three-month and
six-month follow-up intervals.[1]

Overall completion rates in the tests were adequate, but could stand improvement. Pre-service and follow-up information was obtained on 66 percent
of the Chesapeake clients (104 out of 157). Reasons for noncompletion for
the remaining 34 percent were refused either initial consent, pre-service
interview, or follow-up interview (17 percent); could not be located or had
moved out of the area (16 percent); caseworker recommended against interviewing (1 percent). In Durham County, pre-service and follow-up information was
obtained on 61 percent of the clients (54 out of 88). Reasons for noncompletion for the remaining 39 percent were refused (19 percent); could not be located or had left the area (16 percent); caseworker recommended against interviewing (1 percent); no attempt made to follow up due to recordkeeping error
(3 percent).

The overall completion rate is critical. If many clients are "lost" from
the monitoring sample, and if these clients' outcomes are substantially different from those of clients that participate in monitoring, then the monitoring data will not be representative of all clients. Overall completion rates
of about 60 to 65 percent, such as those obtained in the pilot tests, are far
from ideal, although findings even on this proportion of clients should be
useful. Agencies using these procedures should periodically review overall
completion rates. If these drop below about 60 percent, the procedures should
be reassessed and improved.

Chapter 3 includes suggestions for improving the completion rates. We
also recommend that agencies routinely compare the characteristics of participants and nonparticipants (using agency record data) to determine whether
particular groups of clients are not being adequately represented in the outcome data and to consider this when using the data. We compared the demographic characteristics and severity of problems at intake of clients who completed both pilot test interviews with those of clients who did not. There
were only small differences. The two groups differed, however, in amount of
service received, with completers having received greater amounts of service
than noncompleters. If this pattern holds, it will be advisable to analyze
and present outcomes separately by amount of service.

_____

1. Alfred H. Schainblatt et al., Mental Health Services: What Happens
to the Clients? (Washington, D.C.: The Urban Institute, 1979).

## IMPLEMENTATION AND COST OF OUTCOME
## MONITORING PROCEDURES (CHAPTER 4)

Introduction of these outcome monitoring procedures probably won't be easy. Structured interviewing of clients by nonprofessional staff before and after services may be greeted with initial skepticism. The usual lack of strong analytical capability in local social service agencies adds to the difficulty of introducing and sustaining outcome monitoring. Managers' unfamiliarity with the use of outcome data is also an obstacle to its collection and utilization.

Based on the pilot tests, we estimate that regularly assessing what happens to clients in a local agency would require about 2-3/4 to 3-1/2 employee years of effort (approximately forty thousand to fifty thousand dollars annually) for a sample of clients that resulted in completed pre-service and follow-up interviews for 700 to 800 clients (the approximate number of clients that would complete both interviews in an agency with 100 intakes per month in the sample). The largest portion of the cost is for interviewing (two to three full-time interviewers), with the cost of a coordinator's time (approximately one-third to one-half of a full-time professional salary) being the second largest cost. The actual out-of-pocket outlays could be significantly lower if the agency has staff available to undertake some of these activities. These costs do not reflect start-up costs. Local agencies should consider obtaining technical assistance when implementing these procedures. The initial costs for technical assistance and for the professional staff time needed to review the questionnaire and adapt the procedures can be offset by doing fewer interviews in the first year and can be at least partially handled without added out-of-pocket expenses.

For a statewide outcome monitoring system that is centrally coordinated, with interviewers paid by the state, we estimate that the cost for an on-going system would be $150,000 to $180,000 annually for a statewide sample which obtained completed intake and follow-up interviews for three thousand clients. Again, the actual out-of-pocket outlay will be significantly lower if staff members are available to implement some of the activities. A larger number of clients would probably be necessary if the state wished to provide data that would also be useful for a large number of individual local agencies. One approach is to obtain adequate subsamples for each of the largest local agencies in the state and for each region from the remaining smaller local agencies. Costs should probably be shared between the state and local agencies.

The cost of these outcome procedures may be a major obstacle to implementation. Out-of-pocket costs are likely to be less than 5 percent of total agency budgets. However, agency managers with little experience with the use of outcome data may be reluctant to fund measurement. None of the different possible approaches to outcome measurement is cheap, although some have lower out-of-pocket costs due to use of records or caseworkers as the data source (but caseworker time is costly and limited and there are "opportunity costs" to using caseworkers). Experience with outcome data will eventually provide evidence regarding its cost effectiveness. In the meantime, agency managers will have to make a judgment as to the cost of information versus the dangers inherent in making program and policy decisions without systematic information on client outcomes.

## USING THE OUTCOME DATA (CHAPTER 5)

The procedures discussed in this report were developed for uses such as the following:

- Needs assessment, resource allocation, budget preparation and justification. These data can provide systematic information on the distribution of client needs, on expected outcomes of services, and on areas where client outcome data indicate that client needs are not being met by current services

- Program evaluation and cost-effectiveness studies. Outcome data and the measurement procedures should be a component of such studies

- Establishment of performance targets for contractors and employees

- Obtaining client input and providing feedback to staff on overall outcomes

- Providing caseworkers with additional information on individual clients

- Development of quality assurance and staffing standards

The pilot tests described here were primarily feasibility tests, conducted with a small number of clients from a few months' intakes, and they did not test utilization of the data. As part of the tests, we did, however, present some illustrative findings to the pilot test agencies, and these findings formed the basis for discussions of possible uses. These discussions supported the expectation that outcome data are urgently needed and will be used. Even the small amount of test data stimulated many questions about service priorities and training. Agency managers were excited about the prospect of having data to support or refute policies that had been made in the absence of systematic outcome data.

## RECOMMENDATIONS

1. States. The pilot test results suggest that these procedures are workable and that they provide reasonably valid, useful data. However, the pilot tests were too small in scope to provide definitive proof of feasibility, validity, and utility. Therefore, we recommend that states interested in using outcome monitoring procedures implement them initially as "operational tests" in two or three local sites. These operational tests, which should last at least eighteen to twenty-four months, should check the costs, feasibility, reliability, and usefulness of the data. Such tests would also help to further improve questionnaires and scoring procedures and could also include some study of sampling approaches for statewide monitoring.

2.  Local Agencies. Operational testing of these procedures will take
    several years, but needs for outcome data are accelerating now. We
    recommend that local agencies try procedures such as these but care-
    fully monitor the procedures, keeping track of response rates,
    quality of interviewing and coordination, costs, and uses made of
    the data. The procedures should be continued only if they can be
    carried out so as to provide data with reasonable quality and if
    the uses of the data make the cost worthwhile.

As researchers, we would like to see more evidence on the costs and validity of the procedures and on the utility of the data generated.

The procedures discussed in this report are far from perfect. They
should be improved as more experience is gained using them and as the general
"state of the art" of social services outcome measurement improves.

Currently, most state and local social service agencies entirely lack
systematic, regularly collected, objective information on client outcomes.
Even partially tested procedures such as those discussed here will provide
better data than what now exists. If outcome data are regularly collected,
with adequate attention given to the data quality control, and if agency officials spend the time and effort necessary to fully utilize the data, then
outcome monitoring will provide vital information on service performance and
will help social service officials make much more effective use of agency
funds.

# ACKNOWLEDGMENTS

The members of the project team would like to thank a number of persons who were advisors to the project or provided reviews of various draft reports: Vicki Anderson, Department of Human Resources, Arlington County, Virginia; Norman G. Angus, Department of Social Services, state of Utah; Ed Baumheier, University of Denver; Gary Bowers, Bowers & Associates; Timothy Brown and John Cordy, Department of Social and Health Services, state of Washington; Charles F. Cain, Department of Human Resources, state of Kentucky; Vee Carnall, U.S. Department of Health, Education, and Welfare, Region V; Reginald Carter, Department of Social Services, state of Michigan; Wayne Chess, School of Social Work, University of Oklahoma; Helen Hackman, Arlington County, Virginia; Nancy Hayward, National Center for Productivity and Quality of Working Life; Jerry Hercenberg, National Council of Community Health Centers; Allen Holmes, Department of Budget and Fiscal Planning, state of Maryland; Peter Jennings, School of Social Work, Virginia Commonwealth University; J. Donald Judy, Legislative Research Commission, state of Kentucky; Thomas E. Lavelle and Lois Anderson, Department of Administration, state of Minnesota; Robert Mowitz, Pennsylvania State University; Ray Pethtel, Joint Legislative Audit and Review Commission, state of Virginia; Patrick V. Riley, Family Services Association of Greater Boston; Russy Sumariwalla, United Way of America; Catherine G. Williams, Department of Social Services, state of Iowa; and William Benton, Gene Durman, Jeff Koshel, Al Schainblatt, Martin Sundel, and Jerry Turem of The Urban Institute.

We also thank the directors and other project staff of the state departments and local agencies that participated in the pilot tests for their support and help with project efforts: Harold Berdiansky, North Carolina Department of Human Resources; W. D. Clark, Director, Chesapeake Bureau of Social Services; Dan Hudgins, Director, Durham County Department of Social Services; Lee Kittredge, North Carolina Department of Human Resources; John Link, Director, Stanly County Department of Social Services; Dorothy Price, Durham County Department of Social Services; Lois Springer, Stanly County Department of Social Services; and Harriett Sutton, Stanly County Department of Social Services.

David Wilson, Doug Henton, and Bob Raymond, Office of the Assistant Secretary for Planning and Evaluation, our project monitors at the U.S. Department of Health, Education, and Welfare, were always extremely helpful.

# CHAPTER 1.

# INTRODUCTION

Government and nonprofit agencies spend billions of dollars on social services. Agency staff and clients spend millions of hours. How are all these dollars and hours spent? What effect do they have on the lives of clients--are clients better off after receiving services than before, and do the clients themselves feel that the services have helped?

Social services agencies have concentrated almost entirely on the first issue--how dollars and time are spent. Statistics are collected on numbers of clients served, types of services delivered, numbers of hours spent interviewing clients, and so on. Such workload statistics are commonly required by funding bodies such as the U.S. Department of Health, Education, and Welfare and state Title XX administrations.

The question of the effects of services on clients has been neglected. This is partly due to the formidable obstacles that confront agencies when they attempt to measure the "impact" of services. Clients often experience more than one problem and may receive more than one service. Many circumstances affect clients and these circumstances may obscure and confound the effects of an agency's services. The social services effectiveness evaluation that has been done generally has involved one-time studies of specific situations rather than ongoing monitoring of the outcomes of social service programs. "Experimental-control group" evaluations which might enable agencies to separate the impacts of services from the impacts of other factors are costly and difficult and pose legal and ethical problems, and such evaluations are therefore rarely undertaken.

Recently, however, a number of social service agencies have begun to seek ways to regularly track the outcomes of their services. They have been confronted by a gap in the state of the art of social services evaluation-- the lack of practical procedures for regular, ongoing monitoring of outcomes for social service clients.

The Urban Institute, with support from the Department of Health, Education, and Welfare, has developed a set of procedures enabling local and state governments to regularly monitor the outcomes of their social service programs. During 1975 and 1976, we studied previous efforts to develop outcome measurement procedures and, working with the North Carolina Department of Human Resources, drafted a client interview questionnaire and tested it with a small sample of clients. At the conclusion of this first phase, we published a report containing preliminary suggestions and a review of past efforts in outcome measurement.[1] In the second phase of the project, during 1977, 1978, and 1979, the client outcome monitoring questionnaire and procedures were pilot tested in two local public social services agencies and partially tested in one other local agency. The Bureau of Social Services in Chesapeake, Virginia, worked jointly with The Urban Institute to develop and test the procedures. The North Carolina Department of Human Resources supervised tests in Durham and Stanly Counties, with assistance from The Urban Institute. These pilot tests led to numerous changes in the monitoring instruments and procedures.

The outcome monitoring procedures presented in this report include the following elements:

- Throughout the year (or in certain months) all clients (or a sample of clients) are interviewed near the time of application or intake-- "pre-service" interviews. The pre-service monitoring interviews are separate from the regular intake casework interviews. They are conducted in person or by telephone, by trained interviewers (who need not be caseworkers) using a structured questionnaire that includes demographic questions and questions about a number of aspects of functioning and well-being.

- The same clients are interviewed again after some specified interval, such as nine months--"follow-up" interviews. These interviews use a structured questionnaire similar to that used for the pre-service interviews. At follow up, the questionnaire also includes questions regarding client satisfaction with the specific services received and with overall service delivery, and client perceptions of how their problems have changed and which services, if any, they feel helped or hindered them.

- Information is obtained from client records regarding types of services provided to each client, amount and duration of services (so that outcomes can be linked to services provided), plus information on placements and abuse which supplements information collected in the client interviews.

- Client follow-up and change "scores" are calculated and linked with information on services provided and on client characteristics to provide information regarding outcomes for clients of various types (different demographic types, clients with different types and severities of problems at intake), outcomes for different programs or facilities, and outcomes for different services and different amounts of service.

---

1. Annie Millar, Harry Hatry, and Margo Koss, <u>Monitoring the Outcomes of Social Services</u>, vols. 1 and 2 (Washington, D.C.: The Urban Institute, 1977).

## The Pilot Tests

The pilot test in the Chesapeake, Virginia, Bureau of Social Services started in May 1977.[1] A working group composed of Chesapeake professional staff and Urban Institute representatives jointly examined a sample of fifty case records to explore whether the draft client outcome questionnaire adequately covered clients' problems and the objectives of services. The questionnaire was slightly modified and pretested with twenty-eight clients. As a part of the pretest, some reliability testing was undertaken—reinterviews of clients, interviews of clients' caseworkers, and case record checks. Following the pretest, the questionnaire was revised again, and then, from late August until the end of October 1977, the pre-service interviews were administered by clerical staff (who were specifically trained to do the structured interviews) to 123 clients who started services during that period and who consented to participate in the outcome study.[2] These same clients were sought for follow up during May and June 1978.

The North Carolina Department of Human Resources initiated pilot tests in one rural county and one urban county: in Stanly County in September 1977 and in Durham County in January 1978. In both counties, members of the state Department of Human Resources evaluation unit, with assistance from The Urban Institute, coordinated the test efforts.

In the Stanly County Department of Social Services, the questionnaires developed in Chesapeake were modified to fit local interests, pretested with sixteen clients, and further revised. There was also some reliability testing similar to that in Chesapeake. Two undergraduate social work students placed in the agency and two social workers employed under the Comprehensive Education and Training Act (CETA) were trained to do the structured interviews. Within a month of the start of pilot test interviewing, however, staff and funding problems not related to the project interfered with the coordination of the outcome pilot test, and it was temporarily halted after two interviews. In April 1978, despite continuing administrative problems, the agency attempted to restart the pilot test and five more interviews were conducted, but the students' terms ended in May 1978, and in an agency reorganization the CETA social workers were assigned to full caseload positions. The agency decided that it could not participate further without funds from the state to pay for interviewers, which the state did not offer at that time.

---

1. The Bureau serves a mixed urban, suburban, and rural population and has an average ongoing caseload of approximately two thousand clients.

2. An additional seventeen clients were given pre-service interviews but were subsequently dropped from the sample because they received no service from the agency due to ineligibility, leaving the area before services, or withdrawing their applications.

Durham County's Department of Social Services,[1] beginning with the questionnaire resulting from the Stanly County pretest, added several questions related to specific service areas and made some modifications in wording, then pretested the revised questionnaire. They did not have local staff available for interviewing. The state made arrangements with the School of Social Work of the North Carolina Agricultural and Technical State University for students to do telephone interviews and recruited volunteers from the community to do in-person and some telephone interviews. Clients were selected from four different intake units--adult services, services to families with children, child protective services, and delinquency prevention (a special program for adolescents). Within the first two units, we tried to select particular types of clients--adult clients in need of health-related services and services to remain in their own homes, and families getting home management and maintenance services, and a special type of brief service termed "information and referral with follow-through" that goes beyond regular "information and referral." Client pre-service interviews began in March 1978 and continued through the end of July 1978 for a total of sixty-four completed pre-service interviews. After difficulties in coordinating the student and volunteer interviewers, the state decided in mid-May to provide paid interviewers to complete the pre-service interviews. Using paid interviewers, Durham conducted the follow-up interviews, a total of fifty-one, in December 1978 and January 1979.

## Organization of This Report

Chapter 2 describes the design of the client interview questionnaire and how it was developed and tested.

Chapter 3 discusses the issues involved in designing procedures for collecting the outcome data--which clients to monitor, whom to interview, how to protect client rights to informed consent and confidentiality, and who should do the client interviews.

Chapter 4 reviews the steps required to start an outcome monitoring system and to maintain and coordinate the ongoing procedures. The issues involved in local versus statewide monitoring are discussed.

Chapter 5 explores the question of how outcome monitoring data can be used in program and policy decisionmaking, and illustrates how outcome data can be used in conjunction with input and service activity data.

Appendix 1 contains an illustrative client outcome questionnaire (the version administered at follow up to an adult or adolescent client), and Appendix 2 presents the rationale for the specific questions included in the questionnaire. Appendices 3 and 4 present the pilot test findings on reliability and validity.

---

1. The Department's service area includes the city of Durham and the surrounding suburbs and countryside. The average ongoing caseload is approximately fifteen hundred clients.

# CHAPTER 2.

# WHAT DATA ARE COLLECTED IN CLIENT INTERVIEWS AND CASE RECORD REVIEWS?

## What Data Should Be Collected?

Title XX of the Social Security Act groups the objectives of social services into five categories--achieving or maintaining economic self-support; achieving or maintaining self-sufficiency; preventing or remedying neglect, abuse, or exploitation and rehabilitating or reuniting families; preventing or reducing inappropriate institutional care; and providing institutional care when appropriate.

From the social work literature and discussions with social work professionals, we identified nine basic dimensions of client problems in functioning and environment which social services seek to alleviate. The procedures collect outcome data on these nine dimensions plus client satisfaction, background information (demographic characteristics and "presenting problem"), and kind and amount of services that clients receive. Thus, our procedures collect data on the following twelve dimensions:

1.  Physical Health

    Although social services do not usually include the actual provision of medical care, social service agencies do help clients to obtain medical services. In addition, if one accepts the premise that social problems often affect physical health, then physical health becomes, at least indirectly, an "outcome" of social services. However, physical health is also very likely to be significantly affected by factors unrelated to the provision of social services.

2.  Performance of the Activities of Daily Living

    Social service agencies are concerned both with improving clients' own ability to perform the basic activities of daily living--shopping, cooking, laundry, bathing, dressing, eating, and so on--and with providing help with these activities when clients are unable to accomplish them. Assistance with activities of daily living may be provided to allow clients who are disabled, chronically ill, or recuperating from acute illnesses to manage in the community rather than being placed in institutions.

3. Physical Abuse

Protective services to adults and children are a major responsibility of public social service agencies. Services protect clients against both abuse and neglect, but we chose to focus on abuse separately, rather than considering abuse and neglect together. The effects of neglect should show up in other outcome areas (such as in physical health and mental distress).

4. Mental Distress

Mental health seems to be generally accepted as an outcome relevant to social services. In identifying mental health outcomes to assess, we avoided such characteristics as "self-image," "self-esteem," and "mood" because they are abstract, they are particularly difficult to measure, and their relationship to functioning is difficult to interpret. Instead, functional symptoms such as tension, anxiety, and headaches were used. These are also simpler to define and measure. We used a set of questions on symptoms of mental distress adapted from the Denver Community Mental Health Questionnaire (DCMHQ), plus questions on loneliness and on suicidal feelings.

5. Alcohol and Drug Abuse

Social services are commonly directed toward alleviating both problems that may lead to alcohol and drug abuse and social problems that result from such substance abuse. The procedures attempt to assess the outcomes of social services in terms both of reduction in consumption of drugs and alcohol and of reduction in problems such as family conflict and work problems that result from alcohol or drug abuse. An issue in outcome measurement of particular concern here is the honesty of client responses; clients may distort or withhold information on issues such as these.

6. Family Strength

This is a more abstract and value-laden dimension. There seems to be little consensus about the meaning of "family strength" and "family stability" or the methodology for measuring these concepts. We used the approach taken by the Family Service Association of America of asking for client perceptions regarding problems that occur in families, such as problems with handling arguments.

7. Quality of Substitute Care

Social service agencies place and maintain a number of clients in substitute living arrangements such as foster homes, group residences, and various institutions. They are directly or indirectly responsible for the quality of care which clients receive in these placements. Although full assessment of the quality of care in placements is likely to require expert "trained observers" (for such characteristics as facility safety), the clients' perception of the quality of care and their satisfaction with it are important "outcomes."

8.  Child Behavior and Parenting

    Child problem behavior may be related to emotional, medical, and de-
    velopmental difficulties and to neglect, abuse, or a variety of other
    family problems.  Some authorities view problem behavior as merely
    the counterpart of deeper-seated psychological or physical difficul-
    ties and would not necessarily regard alleviation of behavior prob-
    lems as sufficient indication of improvement.  However, we elected to
    focus on behavior problems rather than on possible underlying psycho-
    logical difficulties, both because the former are easier to measure
    and because the problem behaviors themselves are often seen by both
    clients and caseworkers as the target of services.

    The instruments currently available for assessing child behavior are
    lengthy and are generally linked to specific age groups and certain
    categories of problems.  For large-scale monitoring, it seems imprac-
    tical to use different instruments for different categories of chil-
    dren, and so we selected a few basic, readily observable types of be-
    havior problems for assessment.

9.  Economic Self-Support and Security

    Although social services (as opposed to income maintenance) are not
    primarily concerned with supplementing clients' incomes, services can
    help clients manage better on what they have, help them learn skills,
    find jobs, and reduce their dependence on public assistance, and at
    times provide emergency financial assistance for food, rent, fuel and
    utilities, and other basic needs.  The adequacy of household finan-
    cial resources, the extent to which clients are employed, and the ex-
    tent of dependence on public assistance were therefore considered to
    be "outcomes" of services.

10. Client Satisfaction

    Clients were asked about whether they saw their problems, if any, as
    having improved or worsened, and whether they attributed changes to
    social services they received.  In addition, they were asked about
    satisfaction with each specific service they received and about spe-
    cific aspects of service quality such as how well staff members
    treated them, lag time between applying for services and receiving
    them, and the accessibility of facilities and their caseworkers.

11. Background Information

    Age, race, sex, level of education, and household composition seem to
    be the basic demographic features relevant to most service categories.
    It also seems important to know the clients' perceptions of their
    "presenting problems" and what services they are seeking.

12. Services Received

    In order for outcome data to be most useful for exploring the impacts
    of services, it is highly desirable that it be linked to data on the
    amount and type of services given to clients.  Thus, information such

as the number and type of units of service should be provided on each client who is covered by the follow-up effort.

An agency may wish to add other dimensions that would provide more detailed outcome data related to specific programs and objectives. For example, an agency with a major program of housing services might wish to add a dimension on housing problems and quality, which might include questions regarding the conditions in clients' housing and problems such as utilities being cut off and eviction. An agency might want to include a family planning dimension with questions on unwanted pregnancy and utilization of birth control. The pilot test jurisdictions, in fact, added questions on birth control and unwanted pregnancy, a general question on housing problems, a question on problems in obtaining medical care, and several other questions related to specific service programs and service policy issues. The procedures are designed to enable jurisdictions to tailor outcome data to their own needs.

## Sources of the Data

The data for each of these dimensions are collected in pre-service and follow-up interviews of clients and from agency records. Exhibit 1 shows the general source of each type of information. Most data are obtained from client interviews. For each dimension, clients are asked about a number of problems and perceptions of their conditions. Clients are asked about their current or recent problems (usually during a specific time frame such as the past month). In addition, a few items are obtained from social service records, such as data regarding incidents of abuse, number and type of substitute care placements, and information on the amount and type of services provided to the client.

Other government records could also verify some client information on factual points. For example, eligibility-unit data on income and employment, employment security department records, school records, and police records might provide data on some points where the credibility of client reports is questionable. However, difficulties and expenses involved in obtaining these records, plus confidentiality considerations, may make using them more trouble than it is worth. These sources were not used in the pilot tests.

In deciding on the primary source for outcome data, besides client interviews, we considered client self-administered questionnaires, case records, caseworker reports or interviews with caseworkers, and interviews of clients and observations of their living conditions by independent professionals (other than their own caseworkers). A lengthy, written, self-administered questionnaire did not seem feasible for a social services client population. We have found that case records are often incomplete, focus on only one or two problem areas rather than the total range of functioning, and contain information on the client's situation only while the client is in service. Having caseworkers provide outcome information on their own clients introduces a possibility of bias which may reduce the accuracy and credibility of the data; it is difficult to obtain comparable ratings when many raters are involved; and it is highly desirable to avoid requiring additional time and paperwork from already overburdened caseworkers. Moreover, when we interviewed a sample of caseworkers whose clients we had already interviewed, we found that caseworkers' knowledge of clients often was limited to one or two problem areas, rather than the full range of problems that the clients reported in the monitoring interviews, and that often caseworkers had not seen the clients for some time before the follow up.

Having social work professionals other than the clients' own caseworkers interview clients and do independent assessments would avoid some of the problems mentioned, but this would be very expensive. Comprehensive diagnostic assessment procedures are a luxury that most public agencies cannot afford even for service purposes, much less for evaluation.

Overall, it seems that clients themselves are the most practical source of reasonably reliable data on client outcomes. Clients are in a sense the "experts" on their own feelings and problems, and they have more up-to-date information than records or caseworkers have. Even though their judgment about their problems might at times be questionable, and their reports might not always be accurate, complete, or fully frank, they still seem to be the best source of data.

Having decided to use client interviews as the primary source of outcome data, we developed a structured questionnaire suitable for use by nonprofessional trained interviewers. This means that the questionnaire does not require the interviewer to make professional interpretations. The questions need to be understandable to clients and call for information that clients possess. For instance, clients are "experts" on their own feelings and satisfaction with services, but not on a casework "diagnosis" or on an agency's service delivery system.

## Services and Problems Covered by Questionnaire

In order to keep the questionnaire fairly brief, we followed certain principles in selecting questions. First, outcomes should be "end" outcomes rather than "intermediate" outcomes. For example, overall physical health is an ultimate outcome, while obtaining adequate medical care is an intermediate outcome. Second, we concentrated on overall outcomes rather than providing an exhaustive set of questions related to any single specific program's objectives. For example, there are a number of family problems that might be addressed in counseling services--marital relations, sharing of family chores, money management, and so on. However, rather than lengthen the questionnaire with detailed questions, we chose a few broad questions regarding family closeness and conflict.

We followed another major principle in designing the client outcome questionnaire. All clients, regardless of "presenting problem," are asked all questions except those which are clearly inapplicable, such as a substitute care question to a client who lives in his own home. The alternative to this "whole client" approach would be to group clients according to problems and service objectives and for each group to assess only those outcomes that are related specifically to the objectives for that group.

The latter approach offers the advantage that a narrower focus on one or two outcome areas allows for the collection of more detailed outcome data in these areas. It also avoids the need to ask clients about problems that they may feel are not directly relevant to the problems for which they are seeking

help.  A major problem with using the latter approach, however, is the difficulty of identifying, at the time of a client's intake, the client's problems
and service objectives.  Identifying clients' problems and service needs is a
complex, ongoing, client-caseworker process that often extends well beyond intake interviews.  Moreover, clients' problems and needs change during the
course of service, and initial objectives are often modified or even abandoned
in favor of new objectives as service progresses.  In addition, clients seldom
fit neatly into goal categories, even ones as broad as the Title XX goal
categories.

Social services clients frequently have multiple problems, receive more
than one service, and are affected by services in several areas of functioning.
At intake, clients included in the pilot test in Chesapeake, for example, although they usually stated a single problem as the reason why they came for
services--"out of work," "could not pay fuel bill," etc.--actually named an
average of four "major problems," encompassing an average of two problem areas,
in their pre-service interviews.  And the problems named by the clients in the
pre-service interviews were frequently unrelated to the problems that they
mentioned when they were asked why they came to the agency.  Of the pilot test
clients, 46 percent received two or more services, and 27 percent received
three or more.

### The Client Outcome Questionnaire

Appendix 1 of this report presents an illustrative questionnaire based on
the results of the development and test efforts to date.[1]  Appendix 2 contains
the rationale for the dimensions and questions.  The procedures, however, are
not tied to any specific questionnaire.  Agencies that use these procedures
could opt for a different questionnaire, but if so, testing of its reliability
and validity would be necessary.

Questionnaires for pre-service interviews were administered in Chesapeake
(140 clients), in Stanly County (7 clients), and in Durham County (70 clients).
The average lengths of pre-service interviews in the three sites were twenty-
four minutes, forty-five minutes, and twenty-five minutes, respectively.
Follow-up interviews in Chesapeake (106 clients) averaged fifty minutes in
length.  The follow-up interviews in Durham (51 clients) were an average of
forty-six minutes in length (but the median length was smaller, forty minutes,
the average being inflated by a few interviews of more than an hour).[2]  Only
one interview was terminated before completion due to client problems with the
questionnaire and none of the interviewers reported any problems with client
"fatigue."  Thus, the length of the interviews does not appear to be a problem.
In fact, a number of clients appeared to enjoy the interviews, particularly
elderly, isolated clients.

---

1.  The questionnaire in Appendix 1 is one of three versions.  It is the
questionnaire that is used to interview adult and adolescent clients about
themselves.  There are, in addition, versions of the questionnaire for interviewing close relatives or friends about adult and child clients who cannot be
interviewed themselves.

2.  The illustrative questionnaire in Appendix 1 is somewhat shorter than
the questionnaires used in the pilot tests.

The questionnaire appears to have reasonable "face validity." It represents a consensus among a number of social workers and administrators as to the possible range of outcomes of social services (a consensus that has held up with only minor differences among the agencies involved in the pilot tests). In addition, its acceptability to clients has been improved and confirmed by feedback from the interviewers.

Besides standard pretesting of the pre-service and follow-up versions of the questionnaire, the pilot tests included a number of special efforts to check the validity and reliability of the questionnaire. A description of these efforts and our findings are presented in Appendices 3 and 4. Overall, the questionnaire appears to provide data with reasonably good validity and reliability.

# CHAPTER 3.

## DATA-COLLECTION PROCEDURES

New clients are given pre-service interviews near the time of intake and follow-up interviews a specified number of months later. This basic procedure encompasses a number of sticky issues as follows:

How should "new clients" be defined?

Who is the "primary client" whose outcomes should be measured?

Who should be interviewed when "primary clients" cannot be interviewed about themselves due to being too young, ill, or mentally disabled?

Who should determine who is the primary client and who should be interviewed in each case?

When during the intake process should clients be given pre-service interviews?

Should all new clients be monitored, or only a sample, and how should the sample be chosen?

When should follow-up interviews be administered?

What procedures will be required to locate clients at follow up?

What overall completion rates might be expected?

How and where should pre-service and follow-up interviews be conducted?

Who should conduct the client monitoring interviews?

What procedures are required to protect clients' rights to informed consent and confidentiality?

This chapter describes how the pilot test jurisdictions handled these procedural questions and offers recommendations on each.


### Defining "New Clients"

Some clients are served by social service agencies on and off over the years. Periodically such clients reach a certain level of self-sufficiency and terminate services, only to return when a new crisis occurs. Some agencies routinely close cases after the termination of each crisis intervention, while others leave cases open for several months. For example, a young mother may request referral to a family planning clinic, then not be seen again until two months later when she asks for emergency assistance to replace clothing lost in a fire. In one agency she might be considered a "new client," while in another she would be an ongoing "old client." Since in monitoring, one is seeking to measure outcomes "before and after" services, the issue is how long a client must be without service in order to be considered a "new client."

In Chesapeake, cases are monitored for three months after the end of service delivery before being statistically closed. Since closed cases are inactive for at least three months, Chesapeake decided to include as "new clients" reapplicants whose cases had previously been closed, as well as applicants who were completely new to the agency.

In the Durham County pilot test, on the other hand, clients with closed cases, handled as new intakes in the family services and adult services units, had frequently been seen by caseworkers within the past three months. Durham decided not to monitor applicants who had been seen in the past three months.

Outcome monitoring, however, need not and probably should not be limited only to new clients. If an agency has a large proportion of long-term active cases, limiting monitoring to new clients will give an incomplete picture of agency outcomes. In Chesapeake, for example, on June 1, 1977, 50 percent of the cases which were then open had been open for longer than twelve months. Agencies might consider supplementing their outcome data for new clients by annually interviewing a sample of clients who have been active in service for longer than twelve months. Alternatively, they might plan to interview all long-term clients or frequent reapplicants every nine months or every twelve months until their cases are permanently closed.

Recommendation. We suggest that cases should be closed or be completely inactive for at least three months before being counted as "new clients" selected for monitoring. Moreover, no client should be included in the monitoring sample more than once every twelve months, even if the client's case is opened, closed, and reopened during that period. We also recommend that agencies check to see what proportion of their cases at any given time have been open longer than twelve months. If the proportion is large, they might consider monitoring long-term clients as well as new clients. Agencies that have a large proportion of "chronic" clients, whose cases open and close frequently, should consider such clients as long-term clients and monitor them annually.

## Selecting the "Primary Client" for Monitoring

People may apply for services for themselves or for others. For instance, a disabled adult may request chore services in order to remain at home rather than go to an institution. A family with an abused child might need protective services. In the first case, the disabled adult clearly is the primary client. The second case is not as clear. One agency might consider one of the parents to be the primary client, while another might label the case with the child's name. In families where several persons receive services, there may be several "named" clients with separate case records. Agencies could choose to measure outcomes for more than one primary client in each family, but the cost of doing several interviews per case would be prohibitive. Most agencies will seek procedures for selecting a single "primary client" in each case for outcome monitoring.

The pilot test agencies all chose to select one client per family for monitoring. In the North Carolina agencies, an adult client was chosen as "primary client" in all cases except when the family contained an adolescent (age fourteen to seventeen), in which case the adolescent client was chosen (the youngest adolescent if there was more than one).[1] If there was more than one adult client of services, the adult was chosen who was most available for interviewing and capable of being interviewed. If a child or adolescent under age fourteen was clearly the primary client, as in a foster care case, then a relative or other caretaker of the child was interviewed about the child. If several children were primary clients in a case, the oldest child was chosen as the subject of the interviews.

Chesapeake used similar guidelines, except that no special effort was made to interview adolescents rather than adults in families where both were clients.

The issue of whom to interview is especially problematical in protective services. Agencies vary in their designations of primary clients--both parents, only the abusing parent (or other abusing adult), all the children, or only those children who have been abused. Durham decided to consider the more available parent (or an abused adolescent) as primary client for monitoring purposes. Chesapeake did not set a rule, leaving it up to the protective services worker to decide which family member to refer for monitoring.

Recommendation. We recommend that in order to keep procedure costs down, no more than one client per family be included in the outcome monitoring sample. In families with several clients, the adult client most available for interviewing (age eighteen or over) should be selected. If there is no adult client in a case, an adolescent age thirteen or older should be chosen for monitoring. If there is no adult or adolescent client over age twelve, a child should be chosen for monitoring and someone close to the child should be interviewed regarding the child. In protective services, a parent should be monitored. Since the interviews include questions about abuse of, or by, anyone in the family, about family relationships, and about problems with all the children, this seems the best way to get a picture of outcomes for the family as a whole. If the person being interviewed is the "abuser," there could be a problem with misreporting on the abuse questions. This problem will be mitigated if the data regarding abuse are supplemented by information from records.

## Interviewing Others When Primary Clients Cannot Be Interviewed

Whenever possible, clients should be interviewed about themselves. The "primary client" for monitoring, however, may be a child or an adult who can't

---

1. This exception was made because of the agencies' special interest in testing the feasibility of interviewing adolescents.

be interviewed (perhaps because of age, illness, or mental disability). In these cases, someone will have to be interviewed about the client.

"Third-person" versions of the questionnaire were developed in the pilot tests for the purpose of interviewing "others" about clients (one version for interviews about a child, another version for interviews about an adult).

At what age is a client too young to be interviewed? Although questionnaires for interviewing young children have been developed and used in other studies, and a number of members of a 1976 advisory group in the first phase of work in North Carolina encouraged the idea of interviewing children as young as five to six years old, neither time nor funding allowed us to develop an outcome questionnaire for young children. For these pilot tests, we decided to interview only adolescents, for whom the basic adult questionnaire needed only minor modifications. Major concerns about interviewing adolescents included the sensitivity of the birth control, drug and alcohol questions, and some of the family-strength questions. Chesapeake and the North Carolina agencies decided to use ages fifteen and fourteen, respectively, as the lower age limit, ages at which most youth are in high school and have reached a certain degree of autonomy. This age limit was considered higher than necessary by some professionals working with delinquent or deviant youth; the delinquency prevention unit in Durham County felt that all of the outcome questions could be asked of ten- or eleven-year olds.[1]

It is important to choose to interview the person who knows the client best, whether this is the spouse or closest friend of a disabled client, the parent or foster parent of a child, or a lawyer, nurse, or other responsible person close to a client. Since the questionnaire focuses on the client's problems during the past month, it is only worthwhile to interview someone who has seen the client during that month. It seems that this type of interview provides less complete and reliable information than what is obtained when clients are interviewed about themselves. However, in the fifty-five Chesapeake pre-service and follow-up interviews that were conducted with persons other than the primary client, only 1 percent of the questions were answered "don't know."

At follow up, as a general rule, the person interviewed about a client should be the same person who was interviewed pre-service. It is possible, however, that the person who was interviewed about a client in a pre-service interview might no longer be in contact with the client by the time of follow up. For example, an aged client might move from the household of one adult daughter to another daughter's household, or a child be placed in a foster home. In these cases, the person now closest to the client should be interviewed. If a client is interviewed about self at the time of the pre-service interview, but is unable to be interviewed by follow up, then the person closest to the client should be interviewed. It might also happen that a client who cannot be interviewed pre-service can be interviewed by follow up. This occurred in two cases in the Chesapeake pilot, and in one of these cases

---

1. A strong case for obtaining feedback from children down to the age of ten is made in Malcolm Bush, Andrew C. Gordon, and Robert Le Bailley, "Evaluating Child Welfare Services: A Contribution from the Clients," Social Service Review 51 (September 1977): 491-501.

Chesapeake decided to interview both the client and the person who had been interviewed at intake.

These situations in which a different person is interviewed at follow up will cause problems in the reliability of the data regarding "changes" in condition from intake to follow up. Different persons may rate conditions somewhat differently. On balance, however, we suspect that such discrepancies will be less serious than the loss involved in getting no interview at all.

Clients may also be unavailable for interviewing due to being jailed or hospitalized. Chesapeake felt that interviewing jailed clients was appropriate and should involve no major problems. It can be argued, however, that the very condition of being jailed is so negative an "outcome" that it over- shadows the other aspects of client outcomes and renders a follow-up interview superfluous. This depends on the reason for the client being jailed; if it is for a minor offense or an offense that occurred prior to receipt of social services, then it would not necessarily be considered a negative outcome. An argument could similarly be made for hospitalization being an overwhelmingly negative outcome, but this too is subject to qualification according to the cause and severity of the illness. Chesapeake decided to interview hospital- ized clients if they were interviewable and they and their families did not object.

Recommendation. We recommend that agencies interview a third person when a primary client cannot be interviewed, provided the third person knows the client well and has seen the client within the past month. There will be somewhat less confidence in the reliability of the interview data in these cases where the client cannot be interviewed. However, the bias introduced by any reliability problems seems less than the bias that would be introduced by entirely excluding small children and all mentally disabled or seriously ill adults, since these groups are likely to form a significant proportion of the social services clientele.

## Determining the Primary Client and Who Should Be Interviewed

In the pilot tests, intake social workers chose the "primary client" and decided who should be interviewed using guidelines such as those just dis- cussed. However, some intake workers objected to adding more paperwork and another task to the complex eligibility screening and crisis intervention process.

Another way to handle these decisions is to have copies of the intake "face sheets" or case records provided by a receptionist or other clerical staff person to the outcome monitoring coordinator, and to have the coordina- tor choose the primary client and interviewee. However, the coordinator will not have as much information on which to base these decisions as would the in- take workers who have interviewed the clients, and so the coordinator may have to ask intake workers for assistance.

There may be sensitive situations where interviewing a client for moni- toring could have an adverse affect on the client. Clients' caseworkers-- whether intake caseworkers or ongoing service workers--can request that clients not be given monitoring interviews. In Chesapeake, for instance, one worker recommended against interviewing an adolescent in a psychiatric hospital ward. If caseworkers requested large numbers of exemptions, however, and it seemed that these exemptions were less related to client condition than to caseworker avoidance of monitoring, it would be advisable to have supervisors review the exemptions.

Clients in protective services are particularly sensitive to intrusion of privacy. Although both Chesapeake and Durham chose to include protective service cases in the pilot tests, caseworkers were asked to judge whether any given client should be interviewed. In Chesapeake all protective service cases were excluded except those referred by their caseworkers; but in Durham County, all protective service cases were included unless caseworkers objected.[1] In none of the cases were there reports of adverse effects due to a pilot test interview.

Recommendation. Intake caseworkers are generally in the best position to determine who is the primary client and who should be interviewed. However, having many caseworkers, whose time is already overcommitted, responsible for referring clients for monitoring may result in inconsistencies and omissions which can introduce unknown bias into the monitoring sample. Therefore, it is preferable for the coordinator of the monitoring procedures to make these decisions, provided intake face sheets or case records contain sufficient information to allow the coordinator to make most decisions without contacting intake workers. All caseworkers in the agency should be informed about what is involved for clients in the monitoring interviews and told that clients can be exempted from monitoring interviews if caseworkers specifically request such exemption.

## When to Administer Pre-Service Interview

An agency should first examine the process whereby a person moves from applicant to service recipient. In most agencies, the first person an applicant meets is the receptionist who takes the applicant's name and presenting problem, checks whether the applicant is new, ongoing, or previously served, and directs the applicant to the appropriate intake worker. The function of

---

1. In Durham, one protective services case was excluded at the caseworker's request, and four protective services clients were referred of which two refused consent. In Chesapeake, eight clients were referred and four refused. Due to the exclusion of some protective services cases, plus the likelihood of higher rates of client refusal to participate and the chance of misreporting on interview questions related to abuse, it seems likely that interview data alone will be insufficient for assessing protective services outcomes. Agencies should keep systematic data on recurrence of abuse in all cases and use data from areawide or statewide abuse reporting systems. If only a small proportion of protective services clients participate in outcome interviews, an agency might consider obtaining outcome data on protective services clients from their caseworkers. Even though in general the possibility of biases and the lack of information on client condition after termination may render caseworker-provided outcome data somewhat less credible and useful than client-provided data, in the case of protective services the client-provided data alone may be too incomplete or inaccurate to be reliable.

the receptionist, while very sensitive, is primarily clerical and is not considered a social work service. Next, the applicant meets with an intake social worker. This first session with the intake worker may take place the same day or, if there is no emergency, the client may be given an appointment for an intake session several days or weeks later. Especially in public agencies, social work theory and practice regarding this intake session may differ widely. In theory, at least, the intake interview demands specialized casework skills--it is the interview in which applicant and caseworker together assess the presenting problem and determine which of the available services are most likely to alleviate the situation and to improve the person's "functioning." There may be improvement in the client's ability to cope due to having discussed the problem with the intake worker, and whether or not the applicant is later determined to be eligible, immediate service may be delivered during or after the intake interview. A case can be made for including all applicants in the monitoring sample and attempting to interview them before their intake interviews in order to measure their conditions before any service is given to them.

Social workers at one of the participating jurisdictions felt, however, that it would be awkward and possibly traumatic for clients to be interviewed before they had at least had their intake interviews. Not only are clients often upset and unsure of whether they will be able to get the help they want, but they are likely to be confused when intake workers ask some of the same questions, and this may adversely affect the intake interviews.

The bulk of the intake session is frequently devoted to filling out forms. These form the basis for determining the applicant's eligibility to receive services. During the following weeks the applicant may also be required to provide documents to verify income. In such cases, a true "intake" interview takes place only after eligibility has been determined and the client begins service. In an agency where little service is delivered until after eligibility determination, it would be reasonable to wait to select and interview clients for monitoring until after they pass eligibility.

The number and proportion of applicants who are ineligible or who drop out before receiving services will also be a factor in deciding whether to include all applicants. In Durham County, for example, ineligible applicants formed a large proportion of intakes. Not only would it be impractical and expensive to include all of them in monitoring, but rejected applicants are likely to be angry or disappointed and therefore reluctant to participate in monitoring interviews. Stanly County intake workers chose not to refer applicants for monitoring until it had been determined whether they were eligible for services. In Chesapeake, of 204 clients who came through intake during the pilot test pre-service phase and were initially included in the monitoring sample, 46 clients (23 percent) were later dropped from the sample because they had either been found ineligible (12 clients) or had withdrawn their applications or left the area or died before receiving services (34 clients). Pre-service interviews were completed with 16 of these persons who subsequently received no services and were dropped from the sample. In Durham, nine of the original sample of ninety-seven (9 percent) were excluded from the final sample because they had withdrawn or been found ineligible before receiving any services.

Recommendation. If the proportion of applicants who are ineligible or leave before receiving services is large (for example, over about 15 percent), agencies should consider waiting until after eligibility determination to select and interview clients for monitoring. They should probably wait until after the intake interview in any case, to avoid possible adverse effects on the client. This will mean that the pre-service interview will not be completed "before" services begin in some cases, particularly in agencies with immediate-service intake interviews. This trade-off seems acceptable, however, if it saves the agency from interviewing large numbers of clients who turn out to be ineligible or receive no services for other reasons.[1]

## Should All New Clients Be Monitored, or Only a Sample, and How Should the Sample Be Chosen?

An agency, especially a local agency, can decide to assess the outcomes of all new clients. This would provide complete coverage and avoid the possibility of sampling error. However, doing both pre-service and follow-up interviews with all clients may be more than an agency can afford.

Another option is to do pre-service interviews with all new clients but do follow-up interviews with only a sample of the clients who had pre-service interviews. This avoids the complications that would be necessary in order to randomly sample incoming cases. It would also avoid the possibility of some clients being treated differently due to caseworkers' knowing that they are in the monitoring sample. This option also provides pre-service interview data that may be useful to clients' caseworkers (caseworkers often must focus exclusively on presenting problem and have no time to explore many of the areas covered in the broad monitoring interview—see Chapter 5).

If an agency decides not to interview all clients, either pre-service or at follow up, it will need to design sampling procedures. Agencies that choose to sample should find it relatively easy to obtain help from experts on sampling.

One possible sampling procedure is "time sampling," in which only clients who apply in selected weeks or months are included. This seems easier for local and state agencies than random number sampling or sampling based on selecting clients with specific personal or service characteristics. If an agency, for example, wanted a 50 percent sample, it could exclude every other week, or every other month. If it wanted to sample two-thirds of clients, it could exclude every third week or every third month. In deciding which weeks or months to exclude, an agency must consider whether there are "seasonality" or "time-of-the-month" biases involved. For instance, there might be a higher proportion of clients seeking emergency financial assistance when utility or

_____

1. An agency might, however, want to obtain some feedback from clients who are ineligible or are requesting services which the agency does not provide, at least to obtain these clients' perceptions of the fairness and courteousness with which they were treated. An agency also might want on occasion to use persons not receiving services as a comparison group to those that did receive services.

rent bills are due, or a higher proportion of clients seeking assistance for fuel during the winter.

States might wish to sample on the basis of geographic region, caseload size, and urban/rural character. For example, a state with seven regions might construct seventeen subsamples: a sample from each of the ten largest agencies,[1] plus a sample from each of the seven regions. Each subsample could be large enough to provide data for local (county or regional) use as well as for inter-county and inter-region comparisons and statewide assessments.

The size of sample required is dependent on the number of subgroups for which outcome information is desired. If only one characteristic, such as age, will be used to group clients at any one time in the analysis, then the neces- sary sample size is determined by the characteristic that has the most sub- groups. For example, if a state wants to subdivide a total sample for one pur- pose into four age groups, for another purpose into ten types of programs, and a third purpose into fourteen geographical areas, then geographical area would be the characteristic which determines sample size. If 100 clients per sub- group were desired (100 is often considered a minimum subgroup size), then the sample would have to include at least 1,400 clients.

If an agency, however, wants to obtain tabulations using more than one characteristic at a time, the required sample size is multiplied. For ex- ample, if a local agency wants to obtain information on ten types of programs for each of four types of clients, with 100 clients in each program-client type subgroup, then the total sample required would be 4,000. For smaller local agencies, however, where the annual number of incoming clients is small, it may not be possible to get 100 clients in each subgroup, but the information may still be useful provided that the sample includes a large proportion of the total number of clients in each subgroup (and this is likely to be the case, since 100 percent coverage is more feasible in a small-volume agency).

To ensure an adequate follow-up sample, it will be necessary to select a larger sample of clients for pre-service interviews than the desired sample size for follow-up interviews. This allows for loss of clients from monitor- ing due to such reasons as client refusal to participate, failure to locate clients, client deaths, and clients that receive no services. The Chesapeake pilot test experience indicates that the number of clients contacted for the pre-service sample may have to be one and a half to two times as large as the number needed for the follow-up sample. (See the following discussion of com- pletion rates in the pilot tests.) It will also be important to identify the demographic characteristics and service disposition of clients who drop out of the sample, so that they can be compared with the remaining clients in order

---

1. Typically, a small proportion of the local agencies in a state will account for a large proportion of the clients or expenditures. For example, in Virginia the ten largest local agencies (9 percent of the local agencies) accounted for about 46 percent of the planned local Title XX expenditures in 1978. Virginia Department of Welfare, Virginia Commission for the Visually Handicapped, "Commonwealth of Virginia Comprehensive Annual Plan for Social Services (July 1, 1978-June 30, 1979) under Title XX of the National Social Security Act," 1978.

to gauge the degree to which the "representativeness" of the sample is damaged by attrition.

Recommendation. We suggest that local agencies administer pre-service interviews to all clients, to avoid the complications involved in sampling at intake and to provide information on clients for caseworker use. At follow up, clients could then be sampled or all clients could be interviewed. If an agency is unable to afford pre-service interviews of all clients, however, we recommend that the pre-service sample be about twice as large as the desired follow-up sample. An agency that decides to sample should obtain technical assistance to help in designing the sampling procedures.

Since it is likely to be infeasible for a state to monitor all clients statewide, we suggest that a state focus its resources on sampling the agencies with the largest number of clients, with lesser coverage of the smaller agencies. Sampling might be done during selected periods of time. Considerable care must be given to the design of the sampling to avoid geographical and temporal biases. Since statewide sampling was outside the scope of the pilot tests, we have no data regarding such attempts.

Whatever sampling procedure is used, the sampling period should probably be spread throughout the year, to avoid seasonal biases. Moreover, we suspect that client outcome monitoring will be most successful if built into year-round agency procedures.

## Administering Follow-Up Interviews

Follow-up interviews can be done either at case closure or at a time after case closure, or they can occur at a fixed time after pre-service interviews. Although it might be ideal to do follow-up interviews at an interval several months after the end of services in order to measure the lasting and delayed outcomes of services, timing follow ups from case closures has several disadvantages. It is more difficult to keep track of case closure dates than of case opening dates. Definitions of case closure vary, as do caseworkers' applications of criteria for when to close cases. Cases often remain open long after active services cease. Finally, differing lengths of time between pre-service and follow-up interviews for different clients would complicate comparisons of outcomes. In the pilot tests, therefore, follow-up interviews were timed from the pre-service interviews. Thus, all clients had approximately the same length of time between pre-service and follow-up interviews. A drawback of this approach is that some clients will still be in service at follow up. However, the considerable difficulties in defining closure, and the prolonged length of many service cases, appear on balance to make a fixed interval after intake, such as nine months, a preferable time for the follow up.

When timing follow-up interviews according to length of time since pre-service interviews, it is necessary to decide the best time interval. If an agency wishes to have a large proportion of follow-up interviews occur well after case closure, it will be necessary to make the time interval long enough so that many cases are closed. In Chesapeake (in June 1977) we did a survey of length-of-time-in-service for all cases that had been newly opened during the six-month period January to June 1976:   26 percent of these cases were closed within three months, 45 percent within six months, 59 percent within nine months, and 66 percent within eleven months.   (However, many cases may have been inactive for some time before official closing, so the actual length of time in active service probably was somewhat shorter.)   In an agency whose clients spent lengths of time in service similar to those for Chesapeake, it appears that if follow-up interviews are administered some time after case closing for most clients, the pre-service/follow-up interval should be at least nine months and preferably twelve.   There are problems, however, in attempting follow ups too long after active service terminates:   clients who have been out of service for some time become increasingly hard to locate, clients' memories of services may fade, other circumstances may affect clients' conditions, and the findings will be less timely for current program and budget decisions.   An agency will have to balance these drawbacks of long intervals between intake and follow up against the desire to have as many clients as possible no longer receiving services at the time of follow up.

Some agencies may feel that nine months is too long a follow-up interval for clients who receive short-term services that last only a month or so.   An agency might use a rule such as the following:   Clients whose services terminate within forty-five days of pre-service interviews will receive three-month follow-up interviews, and all others will be followed up at nine months.   Implementation of this procedure requires a review of the status of all cases at three months, or a system for ongoing tracking of case closings.

The pilot test efforts used a seven- to eight-month follow-up interval. A parallel Urban Institute effort in mental health outcome measurement tested both three-month and six-month intervals, finding no significant difference in rates of attrition over these different intervals in one of the two sites and a 10 percentage difference in the other (68 percent completion at three months, 58 percent at six months).[1]

Recommendation.   We suggest that follow-up interviews be conducted a specified number of months following pre-service interviews.   The choice of how many months depends on the average duration of cases in an individual agency.   In the pilot test agencies, about nine months appeared to be a reasonable interval.   Agencies with short durations for most cases might use a six-month follow-up interval.

## Locating Clients at Follow Up

A key technical problem with these client outcome monitoring procedures is locating clients at follow up.   If a large proportion of the clients cannot be located and interviewed, the representativeness of the findings will be questionable.

Several procedures can minimize difficulties in locating clients.   At the pre-service interviews, clients can be asked to give the name, address,

---

1.   Alfred H. Schainblatt et al., Mental Health Services:   What Happens to the Clients?

and telephone number of one or two persons who will know where the client is living. Before the follow-up interviews, current telephone directories can be checked, and "to-be-forwarded" letters can be sent asking clients to contact the agency (especially if no telephone number is available). In addition, eligibility unit records, service case records, or caseworkers can be checked for current addresses and telephone numbers. The coordinator in Chesapeake routinely checked service case records for current addresses and telephone numbers before assigning the follow ups to the interviewers. This procedure is less helpful with clients who have not been receiving services or financial assistance for some time. In Chesapeake, 56 percent of the clients who were candidates for follow-up interviews had last seen a caseworker more than a month before the beginning of Chesapeake's follow-up interviewing effort, with 30 percent either formally closed or in the monitoring file. All of the eleven clients that were not contacted for follow up because they had left the area or could not be located had last seen caseworkers more than a month before the start of the follow-up effort.

Once the current telephone number or address is obtained, several calls or trips will often be necessary before clients can be contacted to complete interviews. Exhibit 2 shows, for Chesapeake, the number of telephone calls and trips to clients' homes required to contact clients and either complete interviews or ascertain that clients were unwilling or unable to complete interviews. Nearly two-thirds were contacted without the necessity for home visits, but contacting the remaining third of the cases involved time-consuming travel to clients' or relatives' homes. A large proportion of interviews that were completed by telephone required several telephone calls.

Exhibit 3 shows the number of telephone calls and visits made in the Durham follow-up effort. A much higher proportion of cases than in Chesapeake, about 70 percent, involved trips. Unfortunately, we do not know whether these trips were necessary. Follow-up interviewers were not instructed to avoid trips, and the interviewers preferred to travel to clients' homes and interview them in person. As in Chesapeake, most cases required more than two calls and some of the follow-up efforts involved considerable persistence by interviewers, including multiple calls and trips.

### Completion Rates of Interviews

Exhibit 4 shows the rates of consent and interview completion for Chesapeake. Of 157 clients included in the Chesapeake sample, both pre-service and follow-up data were obtained for 104 clients, for a 66 percent "overall completion rate."[1] This figure of 104 includes 4 clients who participated in the

---

1. This sample of 157 excludes 46 clients who received no services due to ineligibility (12 clients) and leaving the area before services or withdrawing their applications (34 clients), and therefore were dropped from the initial sample of 204 clients. One other client, who was receiving adoption services, was also excluded because the case was atypical among agency services and there were no other adoption cases in the sample. Most of these clients could not be excluded immediately at intake, however, since it was not possible to know in advance that they would receive no services. Therefore,

(continued)

EXHIBIT 2

NUMBER OF TELEPHONE CALLS AND HOME VISITS UNDERTAKEN TO
CONTACT AND INTERVIEW CLIENTS AT FOLLOW UP:  <u>CHESAPEAKE</u>

| Number of Telephone Calls and Home Visits Required | Interviews Completed by Telephone or in the Office[a]<br><br>Number and Cumulative Percentage | Interviews Completed at Clients' Homes<br><br>Number and Cumulative Percentage | Clients Sought but not Interviewed[b]<br><br>Number and Cumulative Percentage | Total All Clients Sought for Follow Up<br><br>Number and Cumulative Percentage |
|---|---|---|---|---|
| 1 call, no home visits | 23 (32%) | -- | 6 (38%) | 29 (24%) |
| 2 calls, no home visits | 12 (49%) | -- | 2 (50%) | 14 (36%) |
| 3 calls, no home visits | 6 (57%) | -- | 1 (56%) | 7 (42%) |
| 4 calls, no home visits | 8 (68%) | -- | 0 | 8 (49%) |
| 5 or more calls, no home visits | 15 (89%) | -- | 4 (81%) | 19 (65%) |
| 1 home visit[c] | 5 (96%) | 12 (39%) | 2 (94%) | 19 (81%) |
| 2 home visits[c] | 1 (97%) | 14 (84%) | 0 | 15 (93%) |
| 3 home visits[c] | 2 (100%) | 1 (87%) | 1 (100%) | 4 (97%) |
| 4 or more home visits[c] | 0 | 4 (100%) | 0 | 4 (100%) |
| Total cases[d] | 72 | 31 | 16 | 119 |

a. Although these interviews were eventually completed by telephone or at the agency office, several required home visits in order to reach the client and set up the interview, or to obtain written consent.

b. These cases include 7 clients that refused the follow-up interview and 4 that were found deceased or too ill to participate.  The remaining 5 clients were not located or had moved out of state.

c. Most of the cases that involved home visits also involved a number of telephone calls, an average of 5 for interviews completed by telephone and 1 for interviews completed by home visit.  The calls were attempts to find the clients or set up appointments for the interviews.

d. There was a total of 74 telephone and office interviews, 32 home interviews, and 25 clients contacted but not interviewed; the figures in this table are smaller because information was missing regarding contact efforts for 12 clients.

EXHIBIT 3

## NUMBER OF TELEPHONE CALLS AND HOME VISITS UNDERTAKEN
## TO CONTACT AND INTERVIEW CLIENTS AT FOLLOW UP:   DURHAM

| Number of Telephone Calls and Home Visits Required | Interviews Completed by Telephone or in the Office[a]<br><br>Number and Cumulative Percentage | Interviews Completed at Clients' Homes<br><br>Number and Cumulative Percentage | Clients Sought but not Interviewed[b]<br><br>Number and Cumulative Percentage | Total All Clients Sought for Follow Up<br><br>Number and Cumulative Percentage |
|---|---|---|---|---|
| 1 call, no home visits | 4 (20%) | -- | 0 | 4 (7%) |
| 2 calls, no home visits | 3 (35%) | -- | 0 | 3 (12%) |
| 3 calls, no home visits | 5 (60%) | -- | 1 (14%) | 6 (22%) |
| 4 calls, no home visits | 0 | -- | 1 (29%) | 1 (24%) |
| 5 or more calls, no home visits | 3 (75%) | -- | 0 | 3 (29%) |
| 1 home visit[c] | 1 (80%) | 15 (48%) | 1 (43%) | 17 (59%) |
| 2 home visits[c] | 2 (90%) | 10 (81%) | 2 (71%) | 14 (83%) |
| 3 home visits[c] | 2 (100%) | 3 (90%) | 2 (100%) | 7 (95%) |
| 4 or more home visits[c] | 0 | 3 (100%) | 0 | 3 (100%) |
| Total cases | 20 | 31 | 7 | 58 |

a. Although these interviews were eventually completed by telephone or at the agency office, several required home visits in order to reach the client and set up the interview, or to obtain written consent.

b. These cases included 1 client that refused the follow-up interview and 6 that were not located or had moved out of the area.

c. Most of the cases that involved home visits also involved a number of telephone calls, an average of 5 for interviews completed by telephone and 2 for interviews completed by home visit.  The calls were attempts to find the clients or set up appointments for the interviews.

EXHIBIT 4

CHESAPEAKE: RATES OF CONSENT AND COMPLETION

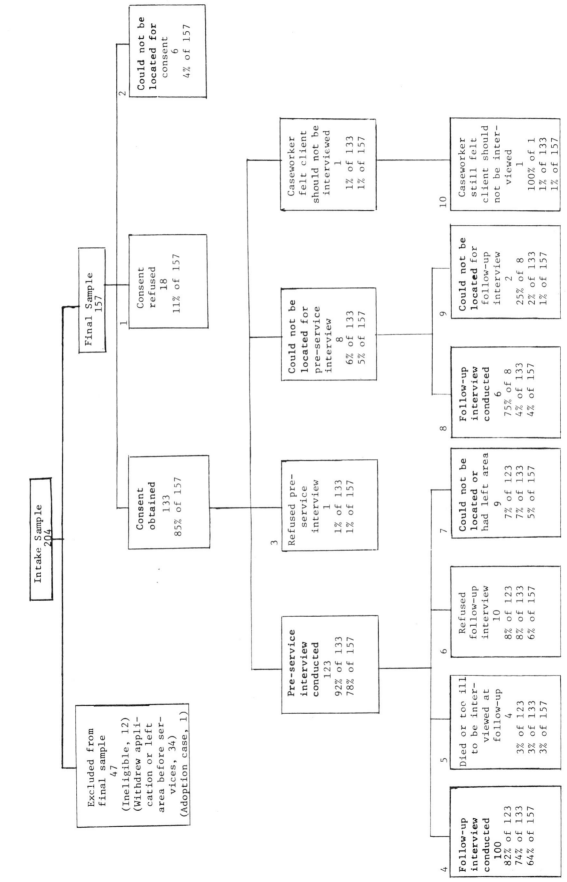

pre-service interview but had died or become severely ill by the time of follow up. These cases were counted as having follow-up data on the assumption that their deaths or illnesses can in themselves be considered as "outcomes."

Of the fifty-three clients that were "lost" from the sample, twenty-nine clients (55 percent of those lost) refused, either initially, before the pre-service interview, or before the follow-up interview (boxes 1+3+6 in Exhibit 4). One client, a hospitalized adolescent, was not interviewed at the caseworker's request (box 10), and the remaining twenty-three clients (43 percent of those lost) could not be contacted, either for initial consent, for the pre-service interview, or for the follow-up interview (boxes 2+7+8+9). Of the six clients not located for consent, one had moved since intake, and five were employed and/or in the WIN program and could not be contacted during working hours. Of the eight clients who consented but were not located for pre-service interviews, two were in the WIN program and unavailable during daytime hours. Of the nine clients who had pre-service interviews but could not be contacted for follow-up interviews, five were known to have left the area, and the remainder were not located at all.

The percentage of clients that completed the pre-service interview but could not be contacted for follow up was relatively small (7 percent of those with a pre-service interview). This indicates that the seven to eight month time lapse did not cause major problems in locating clients. (Social service agencies with higher percentages of shorter term cases might, however, have more difficulty.)

Exhibit 5 shows the rates of consent and interview completion for Durham. Their completion rates were lower, with pre-service and follow-up data obtained on 61 percent of the sample of eighty-eight clients, including three who died (compared to Chesapeake's 66 percent completion rate). Durham completed pre-service interviews for 73 percent of the clients in the sample (compared to Chesapeake's 78 percent) and completed follow-up interviews with 80 percent of those clients who had completed pre-service interviews (nearly the same as Chesapeake). The difference in the percentage completing pre-service interviews mostly results from a higher rate of refusals in Durham (17 percent versus 12 percent). Forty percent of the fifteen refusals were clients from a single caseworker, 86 percent of whose clients refused. None of the other caseworkers had more than 20 percent of their clients refuse, except for a protective services worker, for whom two of four clients refused. Another

_____

(continued)

consents were sought from them, and seventeen were interviewed. The cost of oversampling to compensate for this problem and interviewing some clients who later turn out to receive no services should be figured into the costs when pre-service interviews are done at or near the time of initial application for services.

It is desirable, however, for agencies to know the reasons why clients did not receive services and possibly what happened to them after they withdrew or were turned away. Special procedures such as mailing out brief questionnaires to find out why clients did not receive services and how they feel about the agency seem desirable.

EXHIBIT 5

DURHAM: RATES OF CONSENT AND COMPLETION

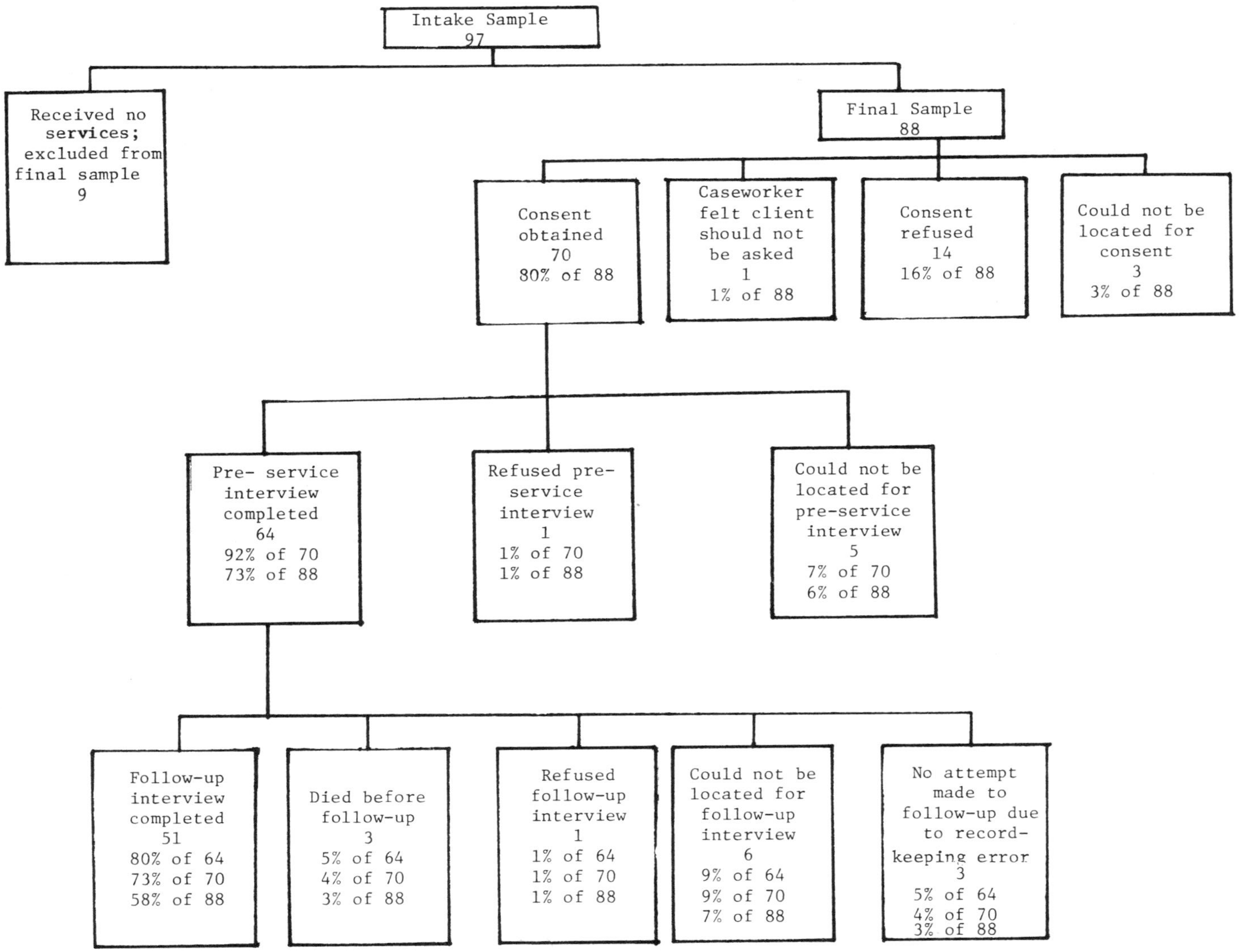

Intake Sample
97

Received no
services;
excluded from
final sample
9

Final Sample
88

Consent
obtained
70
80% of 88

Caseworker
felt client
should not
be asked
1
1% of 88

Consent
refused
14
16% of 88

Could not be
located for
consent
3
3% of 88

Pre-service
interview
completed
64
92% of 70
73% of 88

Refused pre-
service
interview
1
1% of 70
1% of 88

Could not be
located for
pre-service
interview
5
7% of 70
6% of 88

Follow-up
interview
completed
51
80% of 64
73% of 70
58% of 88

Died before
follow-up
3
5% of 64
4% of 70
3% of 88

Refused
follow-up
interview
1
1% of 64
1% of 70
1% of 88

Could not be
located for
follow-up
interview
6
9% of 64
9% of 70
7% of 88

No attempt
made to
follow-up due
to record-
keeping error
3
5% of 64
4% of 70
3% of 88

factor in the lower participation rates for Durham may be that Durham included a group of low-service "Information and Referral with Follow-Through" clients in the study, while Chesapeake excluded such clients. These minimal service clients represented 36 percent of the total sample in Durham, but were 46 percent of the clients who failed to complete both interviews. If these clients were excluded altogether from the consent and completion rates, Durham would have had a completion rate of 64 percent, a rate close to Chesapeake's.

The overall completion rate is a critical issue. If many clients are "lost" from the monitoring sample, and if these clients' outcomes are substantially different from those of clients that participate in monitoring, then the monitoring data will not be representative of all clients.

One way to obtain a partial indication of how participants differ from nonparticipants is to compare data on available characteristics such as age, sex, race, and presenting problem.

Exhibits 6 and 7 show, for the Chesapeake and Durham pilot test clients, comparisons of characteristics of clients who completed both pre-service and follow-up interviews with the characteristics of clients who did not complete both interviews. The two groups do not differ greatly in demographic characteristics. In Chesapeake, there was a slightly higher proportion of white clients among the noncompleters, but in Durham there was a slightly higher proportion of black clients among noncompleters. In Durham, noncompleters were somewhat more highly educated than completers of both interviews, but in Chesapeake the two groups were similar in educational level.

The comparison of client condition at intake also does not give any indication of a significant difference between those completing both interviews and those only completing the intake interview, at least for the small samples included in the pilot tests.

There were, however, differences between completers and noncompleters in the duration of service and in the status of the cases at follow up. In Chesapeake, 13 percent of those who completed both interviews had had three months or less of service, compared to 23 percent of those who did not complete both interviews. In Durham, the corresponding figures were 66 percent and 79 percent, respectively. In Chesapeake, 62 percent of the clients who completed both interviews were still receiving services at the time of follow up, compared to 40 percent of the noncompleters, while in Durham 27 percent of the completers of both interviews were still receiving services, compared to 13 percent of the noncompleters. There seems to be a systematic pattern of somewhat higher rates of dropout from monitoring among clients who receive less service. Although one might argue that an agency can be less concerned about the outcomes of clients that receive very little service, the agency still should be concerned about the outcomes of such clients. (A short mail questionnaire focusing on reasons for not receiving services and client satisfaction with treatment by the agency could be used to obtain information on brief-service clients that do not participate in full-scale monitoring.)

In any case, even if there were substantial differences between completers and noncompleters, the differences can be partly compensated for by presenting the outcome data broken out by specific characteristics. As we

## EXHIBIT 6

## COMPARISONS OF COMPLETERS AND NONCOMPLETERS, CHESAPEAKE

| Characteristic | All Clients In the Study n=157 % | (N) | Clients Who Completed Both Pre-Service and Follow-up Interviews n=100 % | (N) | Clients Who Failed to Complete Both Interviews[a] n=57 % | (N) |
|---|---|---|---|---|---|---|
| **Sex** | | | | | | |
| Male | 18% | (29) | 18% | (18) | 19% | (11) |
| Female | 82 | (128) | 82 | (82) | 81 | (46) |
| | 100% | (157) | 100% | (100) | 100 | (57) |
| **Age** (at intake) | | | | | | |
| 0-17 | 14% | (22) | 14% | (14) | 14% | (8) |
| 18-34 | 43 | (67) | 47 | (47) | 35 | (20) |
| 35-64 | 28 | (44) | 25 | (25) | 33 | (19) |
| 65+ | 15 | (24) | 14 | (14) | 18 | (10) |
| | 100% | (157) | 100% | (100) | 100 | (57) |
| **Race** | | | | | | |
| White | 41% | (65) | 38% | (38) | 47% | (27) |
| Black | 58 | (91) | 61 | (61) | 53 | (30) |
| Other | 1 | (1) | 1 | (1) | 0 | (0) |
| | 100% | (157) | 100% | (100) | 100% | (57) |
| **Marital Status** (at intake) | | | | | | |
| Never married | 30% | (44) | 34% | (32) | 22% | (12) |
| Married | 10 | (15) | 5 | (5) | 18 | (10) |
| Separated or divorced | 42 | (63) | 43 | (43) | 42 | (23) |
| Widowed | 17 | (26) | 17 | (16) | 18 | (10) |
| Other | 1 | (1) | 1 | (1) | 0 | (0) |
| | 100% | (149) | 100% | (94) | 100% | (55) |
| Not applicable (children) | | (8) | | (6) | | (2) |
| **Education** (adults only) | | | | | | |
| Less than 6 years | 17% | (22) | 14% | (12) | 24% | (10) |
| 6-11 years | 54 | (68) | 57 | (49) | 48 | (19) |
| High school diploma or GED | 21 | (26) | 21 | (18) | 20 | (8) |
| Some college or technical | 8 | (10) | 8 | (7) | 8 | (3) |
| College degree | 0 | (0) | 0 | (0) | 0 | (0) |
| | 100% | (126) | 100% | (86) | 100% | (40) |
| Not applicable (children) | | (20) | | (13) | | (7) |
| Unknown | | (11) | | (1) | | (10) |

| Characteristic | All Clients In the Study n=157 % | (N) | Clients Who Completed Both Pre-Service and Follow-up Interviews n=100 % | (N) | Clients Who Failed to Complete Both Interviews[a] n=57 % | (N) |
|---|---|---|---|---|---|---|
| **Location** | | | | | | |
| Rural/suburban, far from agency | 8% | (13) | 7% | (7) | 11% | (6) |
| Rural/suburban, near agency | 31 | (48) | 31 | (30) | 31 | (18) |
| Urban, poor | 53 | (81) | 55 | (53) | 49 | (28) |
| Suburban, middle-class | 8 | (12) | 7 | (7) | 9 | (5) |
| | 100% | (154) | 100% | (97) | 100% | (57) |
| Foster children out of local area | | (3) | | (3) | | |
| **Service Area** | | | | | | |
| Family & child welfare | 41% | (64) | 43% | (43) | 37% | (21) |
| Adult | 37 | (59) | 37 | (37) | 38 | (22) |
| Foster care (child) | 6 | (9) | 6 | (6) | 5 | (3) |
| Protective (child) | 5 | (8) | 3 | (3) | 9 | (5) |
| WIN | 11 | (17) | 11 | (11) | 11 | (6) |
| | 100% | (157) | 100% | (100) | 100% | (57) |
| **Duration of Service** (at time of follow-up interview) | | | | | | |
| 0-3 months | 17% | (26) | 13% | (13) | 23% | (13) |
| 4-6 months | 17 | (26) | 15 | (15) | 20 | (11) |
| 7-9+ months | 66 | (104) | 72 | (72) | 57 | (32) |
| | 100% | (156) | 100% | (100) | 100% | (57) |
| Unknown | | (1) | | | | (1) |
| **Status of Case at Time of Follow-up** | | | | | | |
| Active | 54% | (85) | 62% | (62) | 40% | (23) |
| Inactive or closed | 46 | (72) | 38 | (38) | 60 | (34) |
| | 100% | (157) | 100% | (100) | 100% | (57) |
| **Problem Level at Intake (Overall)[b]** | n=123[c] | | n=100 | | n=23[c] | |
| 0-3 | 9% | (11) | 7% | (7) | 17% | (4) |
| 4-7 | 33 | (41) | 35 | (35) | 26 | (6) |
| 8-11 | 22 | (27) | 23 | (23) | 17 | (4) |
| 12-15 | 23 | (28) | 21 | (21) | 31 | (7) |
| 16-19 | 13 | (16) | 14 | (14) | 9 | (2) |
| | 100% | (123) | 100% | (100) | 100% | (23) |

a. Includes 19 clients who refused initial consent or the initial interview, 7 clients who could not be contacted initially or whose caseworker advised against participation, 6 clients who could not be contacted for the initial interview but who had a follow-up interview, 2 clients who consented but could not be contacted for either interview, and 23 clients who had intake but not follow-up interviews.

b. These are overall scores for the entire pre-service questionnaire. Low scores represent less serious problems. The range of scores was roughly broken into 5 ranges for the purpose of comparing the two groups of completers and noncompleters.

c. Includes only those clients who completed pre-service interviews.

## EXHIBIT 7

### COMPARISONS OF COMPLETERS AND NONCOMPLETERS, DURHAM

| Characteristic | All Clients In the Study n=88 % | (N) | Clients Who Completed Both Pre-Service and Follow-up Interviews n=51 % | (N) | Clients Who Failed to Complete Both Interviews[a] n=37 % | (N) |
|---|---|---|---|---|---|---|
| **Sex** | | | | | | |
| Male | 16% | (13) | 12% | (6) | 22% | (7) |
| Female | 84 | (70) | 88 | (45) | 78 | (25) |
| | 100% | (83) | 100% | (51) | 100% | (32) |
| Unknown | | (5) | | | | (5) |
| **Age (at intake)** | | | | | | |
| 0-17 | 1% | (1) | 0% | (0) | 3% | (1) |
| 18-34 | 55 | (46) | 49 | (25) | 66 | (21) |
| 35-64 | 28 | (23) | 31 | (16) | 22 | (7) |
| 65+ | 16 | (13) | 20 | (10) | 9 | (3) |
| | 100% | (83) | 100% | (51) | 100% | (32) |
| Unknown | | (5) | | | | (5) |
| **Race** | | | | | | |
| White | 22% | (18) | 25% | (13) | 16% | (5) |
| Black | 78 | (65) | 75 | (38) | 84 | (27) |
| | 100% | (83) | 100% | (51) | 100% | (32) |
| Unknown | | (5) | | | | (5) |
| **Marital Status (at intake)** | | | | | | |
| Never married | 27% | (22) | 25% | (13) | 30% | (9) |
| Married | 17 | (14) | 16 | (8) | 20 | (6) |
| Separated or divorced | 42 | (34) | 43 | (22) | 40 | (12) |
| Widowed | 14 | (11) | 16 | (8) | 10 | (3) |
| | 100% | (81) | 100% | (51) | 100% | (30) |
| Not applicable (children) | | (1) | | (0) | | (1) |
| Unknown | | (6) | | (0) | | (6) |
| **Education (adults only)** | | | | | | |
| Less than 6 years | 8% | (5) | 8% | (4) | 9% | (1) |
| 6-11 years | 48 | (29) | 52 | (25) | 36 | (4) |
| High school diploma or GED | 15 | (9) | 16 | (8) | 9 | (1) |
| Some college or technical | 27 | (16) | 24 | (12) | 36 | (4) |
| College degree | 2 | (1) | 0 | (0) | 9 | (1) |
| | 100% | (60) | 100% | (49) | 99% | (11) |
| Not applicable (children) | | (1) | | (0) | | (1) |
| Unknown | | (27) | | (2) | | (25) |

| Characteristic | All Clients In the Study n=88 % | (N) | Clients Who Completed Both Pre-Service and Follow-up Interviews n=51 % | (N) | Clients Who Failed to Complete Both Interviews[a] n=37 % | (N) |
|---|---|---|---|---|---|---|
| **Service Area** | | | | | | |
| Home management & maintenance | 41% | (36) | 49% | (25) | 30% | (11) |
| Information and referral with follow-through | 36 | (32) | 29 | (15) | 46 | (17) |
| Protective Services for children | 6 | (5) | 2 | (1) | 11 | (4) |
| Adult health services and/or services to remain in own home | 17 | (15) | 20 | (10) | 13 | (5) |
| | 100% | (88) | 100% | (51) | 100% | (37) |
| **Duration of Service** | | | | | | |
| 0-3 months | 71% | (57) | 66% | (34) | 79% | (23) |
| 4-6 months | 11 | (9) | 14 | (7) | 7 | (2) |
| 7-9+ months | 18 | (14) | 20 | (10) | 14 | (4) |
| | 100% | (80) | 100% | (51) | 100% | (29) |
| Unknown | | (8) | | (0) | | (8) |
| **Status of Case at Time of Follow-up** | | | | | | |
| Active | 22% | (18) | 27% | (14) | 13% | (4) |
| Inactive or closed | 78 | (63) | 73 | (37) | 87 | (26) |
| | 100% | (81) | 100% | (51) | 100% | (30) |
| Unknown | | (7) | | (0) | | (7) |
| **Problem Level at Intake (Overall)[b]** | n=64[c] | | n=51 | | n=13[c] | |
| 0-3 | 3% | (2) | 4% | (2) | 0% | (0) |
| 4-7 | 19 | (11) | 17 | (8) | 27 | (3) |
| 8-11 | 29 | (17) | 29 | (14) | 27 | (3) |
| 12-15 | 35 | (21) | 35 | (17) | 37 | (4) |
| 16+ | 14 | (8) | 15 | (7) | 9 | (1) |
| | 100% | (59) | 100% | (48) | 100% | (11) |
| Unknown | | (5) | | (3) | | (2) |

a. Includes 15 clients who refused initial consent or the initial interviews, 4 clients who could not be contacted initially or whose caseworker advised against participation, 5 clients who could not be contacted for the initial interview, and 13 clients who had intake interviews but not follow-up interviews.

b. These are overall scores for all the entire intake questionnaire. Low scores represent less serious problems. The range of scores was roughly broken into 5 ranges for the purpose of comparing the two groups of completers and noncompleters.

c. Includes only those clients who completed pre-service interviews.

discuss in Chapter 5, outcome data should be presented for each demographic subgroup, for example, outcomes for male clients presented separately from data presented for females. When aggregated outcome data are needed, the totals can be adjusted for underrepresentation. For example, if males had poorer outcomes but were underrepresented among participants, then the total outcome figures should be adjusted by weighting each sex's overall outcomes by its proportion of all incoming clients. This would remove the bias on outcomes produced by having an excess of females who had better outcomes. (If there are no differences in outcomes by sex, or other characteristics, then no adjustment is necessary, even if there are large imbalances in representation.)

Such compensatory procedures based on outcomes for different demographic groups do not fully resolve, however, possible biases resulting from clients dropping out of the sample. It is possible that nonparticipants differ in outcomes from participants with the same demographic and service characteristics. For example, the outcomes of nonparticipating males might differ from those of participating males. There is no easy way to discover such differences, since it is difficult to obtain comparable outcome data on nonparticipants. Our current project did not have the resources to make special efforts to seek outcome data regarding clients who did not consent to participate in interviews or were not located during the routine procedures. There have been a few studies by others, however, that have attempted to compare the outcomes of nonparticipants with those of participants. Several found that there were no important differences between participants and nonparticipants, but at least one found some differences.[1]

## Determining How and Where to Conduct Pre-Service and Follow-Up Interviews

Three modes of interviewing were used in the pilot tests: telephone interviews, in-person office interviews, and in-person home interviews.[2] All

---

1. Itzhak Levav and Amos Arnon, "Nonrespondents in a Psychiatric Survey," American Journal of Public Health 6 (October 1976): 989-91; Ronald F. Kokes, William Fremouw, and John S. Strauss, "Lost Subjects, Source of Bias in Clinical Research?" Archives of General Psychiatry 34 (November 1977): 1363-65; Kenneth B. Stein, "Psychotherapy Patients as Research Subjects: Problems in Cooperativeness, Representativeness, and Generalizability," Journal of Consulting and Clinical Psychology 37 (1971): 99-105; and Robert B. Ellsworth, "Does Follow-up Loss Reflect Poor Outcome?" Draft Report. (Salem, Va.: Veterans' Administration Hospital, 1978).

2. We did not try to use a self-administered mail-out questionnaire. We believe that a shortened version of the questionnaire is worth investigating. A shorter questionnaire would reduce interview and some data processing and analysis time (particularly if the latter are done manually). If the questionnaire could be made short enough for mail self-administration, this would save even more--though telephone and perhaps in-person follow ups of nonrespondents would still be needed to obtain adequate completion rates. Our concern, however, is that the complexity and varied nature of social services and of client problems mean that significant shortening could result in the loss of substantive information.

three modes appear to yield equally valid and reliable information, but vary greatly in cost. Exhibit 8 shows the amount of time spent by interviewers in contacting clients (excluding actual interview time). At-home, in-person interviewing is by far the most time-consuming. It is essential when a client does not have access to a telephone and cannot come to the office for the interview. Eliminating these clients from the study could seriously bias the sample. In order to plan interviewing resources, agencies should determine the proportion of clients who cannot be reached by telephone, the proportion of nontelephone clients who can make (or can be asked to make) in-person office visits, and the proportion of clients who have no telephone and cannot be interviewed in the office.

In Chesapeake, 78 percent of the clients who had pre-service and follow-up interviews had their own telephones or could be reached by telephone at the time of intake. Sixteen clients with telephones in Chesapeake, however, were not interviewed pre-service by telephone for the following reasons: client was deaf (one case); client did not answer (two cases); phone number changed (one case); client preferred an office or home interview (four cases); required written consent was not obtained by the intake worker, so client had to be visited at home for consent and was interviewed at the same time (eight cases). Of those clients that had telephones at the time of the pre-service interview, thirteen had to be interviewed in person at follow up, for the following reasons: client was deaf (one case); phone had been disconnected (five cases); phone was a neighbor's phone and not very accessible to client (two cases); client requested in-person interview (two cases); phone number changed (one case); (no reason was given for the other two cases).

In Durham 80 percent of the clients interviewed at intake had telephones (fifty-one of sixty-four). Of these people with telephones, however, eight were interviewed in the office and eleven were interviewed in person in their homes. Durham tried whenever possible to schedule office interviews, and ten of the home visits to clients with telephones were required to obtain written consents from clients referred under a modified procedure whereby caseworkers handed them information letters but did not seek consent (see discussion of consent procedures later in this chapter). One other person who had a telephone preferred an at-home interview. Of those clients who had telephones at the time of the pre-service interview, twenty-four were interviewed in person at follow up, for the following reasons: client was hospitalized (two), client no longer had a telephone (six), client's number had been changed to an unlisted one (one), client preferred not to be interviewed on the friend's or relative's telephone that had been used for the pre-service interview (two), and client had a telephone but the interviewer decided to make a home visit (thirteen). The large number of cases where the interviewers decided to make home visits for the follow-up interview was primarily due to the interviewer's preference for in-person interviews, and in most cases the appointments for the interviews were made by telephone beforehand. In two cases, the home visit was due to being unable to reach the client by telephone. There were two clients who had no telephones at the time of the pre-service interview who acquired them and were interviewed by telephone at follow up.

For those clients who cannot or will not be interviewed by telephone, in-person interviews can be done at the agency offices or at their homes. It is preferable to interview in the office, to save interviewer travel-time

EXHIBIT 8

AVERAGE NONINTERVIEW TIME SPENT BY INTERVIEWERS--
TRAVEL AND TELEPHONE TIME BY MODE OF INTERVIEW

| Mode of Interview | Chesapeake Pre-Service Interviews | Chesapeake Follow-up Interviews | Durham Pre-service Interviews | Durham Follow-up Interviews | Average, All Interviews, Both Sites |
|---|---|---|---|---|---|
| Telephone | 2 minutes (n=82) | 8 minutes (n=73) | 4 minutes (n=32) | 26 minutes (n=20) | 7 minutes (n=207) |
| Office | * | 12 minutes (n=1) | Less than 1 minute (n=11) | -- | 1 minute (n=12) |
| Home Visit | 28 minutes (n=38) | 40 minutes (n=32) | 30 minutes (n=21) | 66 minutes (n=31) | 41 minutes (n=122) |
| Total, all modes | 10 minutes (n=120*) | 17 minutes (n=106) | 11 minutes (n=64) | 50 minutes (n=51) | 19 minutes (n=341) |

*Information on noninterview time is not available for the three clients that were interviewed in the agency office during the Chesapeake pre-service phase.

costs. In Durham, an attempt was made to interview as many clients as possible in the office on the same day as their intake appointments or to make an appointment for them to come to the office at a later date. As a result, 17 percent of the pre-service interviews were conducted at the agency offices. Based on the Durham experience, it appears that in-office interviews are most feasible when the interviewers are full-time employees of the agency, rather than volunteer or part-time interviewers who may not be at the agency when clients come for intake interviews.

Related issues are whether to incur the costs of long-distance telephone calls necessary to interview clients who move away from the area before follow up, whether to arrange work hours for interviewers so clients who work or go to school during the day can be interviewed in the evenings or on weekends (perhaps requiring overtime pay), and whether to pay clients' travel costs to bring them to the agency for the interviews.

Recommendation. We recommend that as many interviews as possible be conducted by telephone. Telephone interviewing appears feasible, and we have no evidence that it provides less reliable data than in person. Arrangements should be made to permit calls in the evening and weekends. For clients that cannot be interviewed by telephone, every effort should be made to interview them at the agency offices, including having interviewers on call in the agency to see clients on days when they are in the agency for other reasons. If necessary, clients' transportation costs can be paid when they must make special trips to the agency for monitoring interviews. When neither telephone nor in-office interviews can be arranged, at-home interviews should be done if this group represents a significant proportion of the agency's clients. Otherwise, the representativeness of the sample will be in severe doubt.

## Selecting Persons to Conduct the Client Monitoring Interviews

The procedures avoid requiring clients' caseworkers to provide monitoring data. There are several reasons for this: (1) Particularly in public agencies, caseworkers are burdened with excessive caseloads and urgent responsibilities for clients. Since caseworkers' first priority is service to clients, they will tend to resist tasks that do not immediately contribute to client care. Also, caseworker time is costly. (2) It is difficult to obtain reliable, comparable ratings when many raters are involved. (3) Caseworkers usually are informed about clients' status only up to the termination of services, so that unless caseworkers made a special follow up, there would be no way for caseworkers to judge how client gains are maintained after service termination. (4) Finally, having caseworkers provide outcome information on their own clients introduces a question of bias that can affect the credibility of the information for evaluation. There is a potential conflict of interest if caseworkers' ratings are used to help evaluate the services they provide.

Caseworkers other than the clients' own caseworkers could be hired or assigned to interview clients for monitoring, thus avoiding the bias involved in using clients' own caseworkers, but this option would be expensive.

Therefore, the questionnaires are designed so that trained interviewers, who need not be caseworkers, can interview clients. The pilot test jurisdictions used a variety of interviewers. Chesapeake trained five clerical workers to do the pre-service interviews. For the follow-up interviews, Chesapeake used one of these clerical workers plus nonprofessional staff members who were employed under the Comprehensive Education and Training Act (CETA). Stanly County also used CETA workers (two). Chesapeake, which has decided to resume the collection of outcome data, has applied for CETA workers to do the interviewing. The interviewing work involved in these procedures is a good training opportunity for CETA employees. Interviewing experience and familiarity with client problems and with social service programs can be useful in other jobs.

Both Stanly and Durham Counties used social work students. The Durham students participated as part of a class research project, while the Stanly students had been assigned to the agency for their regular field placement. In both cases, however, there were scheduling problems due to the students' part-time availability, and they dropped out of the project when the semester ended. Using students seems to be a last resort, since there will be constant turnover as well as availability problems at exam times, semester breaks, and school holidays.

Durham County tried using volunteers. There were problems in finding interviewers and occasional problems with attendance. The volunteers obtained, however, generally were able to do the interviews. However, there were some difficulties in scheduling clients for office interviews when volunteers were available. If the agency can schedule interviews so as to avoid problems due to volunteers not being in the office full time, then dependable volunteers can serve as a useful complement to a basic cadre of agency interviewers. They may be in a better position to do at-home and after-hours interviewing than full-time agency staff.

Durham used paid outside interviewers for some of the pre-service interviews and all of the follow-up interviews. These interviewers were recruited and supervised by state evaluation office staff. An alternative is to contract with a survey firm, which would then handle recruitment, training, and supervision of the interviewers.

In deciding how many interviewers to select and train, an agency should be conservative in its estimates of how many interviews per day an interviewer can accomplish. To judge solely from the time involved in calling and traveling to clients' homes and conducting the actual interviews, it would appear that seven or eight interviews a day should be possible. However, there are difficulties in contacting clients and in scheduling appointments, interviewers need to spend some time with the coordinator who supervises them, they need time between interviews to attend to other work-related or personal needs, and interviewing can be fatiguing and stressful. Therefore, an average of four interviews a day is probably the maximum that can be expected of an interviewer; the pilot test interviewers at times did four interviews per day but usually did fewer.[1] Extra interviewers should be selected and trained to allow for

---

1. The University of Oklahoma, in conducting a statewide outcome study involving client interviews similar to ours in length and difficulty, found that interviewers averaged three to four interviews per day. After having used both interviewers hired onto the staff and interviewers contracted on a per-interview basis they prefer the latter. Turnover due to "burn-out" from the stress of interviewing was more of a problem when interviewers were hired

(continued)

interviewer turnover. The interviewing staff should, however, be as small as possible within these requirements, since problems with quality control and supervision expand with the number of interviewers.

The training of interviewers in the pilot tests included several steps: (1) a basic orientation to the project, its purpose, and the content of the questionnaire; (2) a discussion of general interviewing techniques and guidelines regarding consent, confidentiality, and the handling of sensitive questions and client reluctance to answer;[1] (3) role play of the questionnaire; (4) instruction on the recording and editing of the interview; and (5) a small pretest in which each new interviewer completes a few actual interviews and then reviews them with the instructor before beginning full-scale interviewing. Steps 1-4 were all included in a one-day group session. Step 5 can be done in one-to-one contacts or in a group session. After that, we suggest frequent meetings--at least twice a month--between the coordinator and interviewers to discuss problems encountered in interviewing and scheduling.

The role play is crucial. Interviewers should take turns at being interviewer and interviewee. Not only does this familiarize interviewers with the questionnaire, but it allows them to practice handling some of the difficult situations that arise in actual interviewing, such as client questions about the purpose of the interview or of individual questions and client reluctance or hostility. In the pilot test role plays, the interviewers took great delight in playing extremely uncooperative clients. Interviewers' ambivalence about asking personal questions and their fears about client reactions came out in the role play, facilitating open discussion and clarification. A variety of training techniques can be utilized. For example, the trainers in Durham County conducted some role playing on the telephone with the other trainees listening in on extensions.

Training should also stress full and proper recording of client responses. Not only should answers be circled carefully, but any client comments other than straightforward choices of answer categories should be recorded. Immediately after completing each interview, the interviewer should go over the entire questionnaire, making sure answers and comments are complete and legible.

Regardless of the background of the interviewers, it is important to have interviewers who like interviewing and are good at it. The early role playing and pretest steps should provide opportunities for new interviewers to decide whether they enjoy interviewing, and for instructors to gauge their interviewing potential and current skill.

In the pilot tests, the initial training sessions of one day each were conducted in Chesapeake by Urban Institute staff and in North Carolina were jointly run by Institute staff and staff from the State Department of Human Resources. Subsequently, both Chesapeake and North Carolina handled the training themselves. We recommend that an agency obtain outside assistance in training for the first efforts unless someone in the agency has experience

---

rather than contracted. Personal Communication, Professor Wayne Chess, University of Oklahoma School of Social Work, January 1979.

1. Clients' right to refuse to participate should be stressed. Even a client who has signed a written consent has the right to refuse at any time to answer a question or set of questions or to terminate the interview.

with training nonprofessionals to administer structured questionnaires. Although social workers are, of course, experts in casework interviewing, structured interviewing is quite different.

Recommendation. The two best alternatives for interviewers seem to be either (1) agency clerical or paraprofessional employees hired for or assigned to the monitoring effort and carefully trained; or (2) paid outside interviewers, preferably recruited, trained, and supervised by a contracting survey firm. Students and volunteers may be used to supplement paid interviewers but are not as likely to be available for interviewing on a regular basis. A sufficient number of interviewers should be provided so that no interviewer is required to do more than about four interviews a day. Additional interviewers should be trained to allow for possible attrition. Training and ongoing supervision of interviewers is crucial to maintaining the quality of data.

## Procedures Required to Protect Clients' Rights to Informed Consent and Confidentiality

### Consent

Any client should have the right to refuse to be interviewed or not to answer any given question. Even if the pre-service interview is made a routine part of the intake process for all clients, client nonparticipation should never be a basis for denying services.

In order to assure clients' right to refuse, an agency has an obligation to obtain a client's "informed consent" before conducting an interview. This informed consent must include telling clients the purpose of the questionnaire, telling them who will have access to the information, and explaining that they have a right to refuse to answer all or any part of the questionnaire and this will not affect the services they will receive. This information should be given as simply as possible to assure that it is understood, and to make sure that the client, already besieged by eligibility requirements, does not become further confused. Ethical evaluation practice also requires that the interviewer explain any aspect of the procedure about which the client inquires.

Such informed consent may be written or verbal. It is not clear that an agency-run outcome monitoring project is legally required to obtain signed written consents from clients. Recent recommendations from the National Commission for the Protection of Human Subjects of Biomedical and Behavioral Research indicates that in outcome monitoring, as in most evaluation studies, written consent is not necessary. The National Commission report states, "consent forms should not be considered the only method by which information about the research is communicated to subjects. Usually an oral presentation will be an effective method of communication with subjects. The documentation of consent (i.e., the consent form) should never be confused with the substance of informed consent." The report further states that "the requirement for documentation may place an undue burden on the research while adding little protection to the subjects. Such burdens might include a negative impact on the validity of a survey sample....In many cases (e.g., a survey using mailed questionnaires) it would be appropriate for the investigator to provide subjects with a written statement regarding the research, but not to request their signature. In other cases (e.g., a telephone survey) an oral explanation might be sufficient, because subjects can readily terminate their involvement in the research."[1]

We know of no federal legislation that clearly requires written consents for outcome monitoring, even where federal funds are involved. The wording of legislation and executive branch regulations is ambiguous, and the issue, so far as we know, has not yet been clarified in the courts.

The principles of informed consent should be carefully followed, regardless of whether written or oral consents are used. The National Commission states that it is necessary to do the following:

- Provide subjects with an interval of time (consistent with the nature of the procedure) in which to weigh risks and benefits, consider alternatives, and ask questions or consult with others

- Avoid seeking consent in physical settings in which subjects may feel coerced or unduly influenced to participate

- Avoid seeking consent when subjects are in a vulnerable emotional state

- Properly communicate all information relevant to a decision regarding participation to the subjects

- Indicate to subjects that their questions about the purpose of the questionnaire are appropriate and will be answered

- Indicate to subjects whether the results will be made available to them.

It could be argued that applicants for social services may be vulnerable emotionally and may feel coerced, fearing that despite reassurances services might be affected by refusal. It is important to weigh whether any given client is truly capable of informed consent, or whether the request should be postponed until the client is capable, or whether someone other than the client should be asked for consent and interviewed. In addition to the opportunity to refuse initial consent, clients have additional explicit opportunities to refuse at the time of the pre-service interview (if it is conducted at a different time than the consent) and at the time they are contacted for follow up. This does not relieve the agency of the responsibility to be sure that initial consent is truly "informed," but it does further protect the clients' rights.

For the pilot tests, the three jurisdictions were told by their legal advisors that written consent should be obtained from clients before pre-service interviews. In making this requirement, they cited the involvement of The

---

1. National Commission for the Protection of Human Subjects of Biomedical and Behavioral Research, "Institutional Review Boards; Report and Recommendations," _Federal Register_, vol. 43, no. 231 (1978): 5681.

Urban Institute (an outside firm not included in blanket confidentiality
releases allowing in-house staff to exchange information) and the fact that
this was a feasibility study, not likely to have a direct impact on improving
service to the particular clients in the study. The resulting procedures required to obtain consents were quite troublesome and expensive, as described
next. We hope that agencies will not be required to obtain written consents
for regular outcome monitoring.

All three local agencies initially used basically the same consent procedure. At the intake interview, if clients were interviewed in person, they
were asked by the intake worker to sign written consent forms. Exhibit 9 illustrates the consent form used in the pilot tests. If clients were not seen
in person for intake or if the intake worker failed to ask clients to sign the
consents, then interviewers sought consents at a later time, usually making
special trips to clients' homes.

In Chesapeake, 57 percent of the clients were asked for consent by the
intake workers. The remainder of the consents were sought by members of the
interviewing team, who made home visits to clients. These visits took an
average of twenty-six minutes of extra time, largely travel time. Of the clients who had to be visited at home for consents, 63 percent had telephones and
therefore would not have required home visits for consent if written consents
had not been required. The rate of refusal was considerably lower where intake workers handled the consents (10 percent refused) than where interviewers
made home visits (23 percent refused). Another 14 percent of clients whose
consents were sought by interviewers could not be located for consent, so that
the overall rate of consent was 63 percent for interviewers as against 90 percent for caseworkers. An additional problem arose because in many cases someone was sent out to get a number of consents at a time, rather than having
interviewers request consents and conduct interviews at the same time. In
these cases an additional week or two was added to the lapse of time between
intake and the pre-service interview, raising questions as to whether the
"pre-service" interview took place before substantial services were delivered.

In all three test agencies, having intake workers administer consents and
refer clients for monitoring proved problematical. In each agency, there were
a large number of workers in different units who had to be oriented to the
project and the consent procedure. Caseworkers sometimes forgot to request
consents. Also, some clients did not apply in person, so that caseworkers
were not able to get written consents. In Stanly County, for example, there
were intake units in the central office, the hospital, and the health department. In Durham, each service unit had its own intake. In addition to problems in orienting so many workers to the consent process and maintaining consistent, steady referrals, the intake workers themselves were somewhat unhappy
with the procedures. They felt that the time required to get consent could
cut a sizable hole in the crucial intake interview. In Durham, workers found
that consent took as much as twenty minutes; in Chesapeake, consents took an
average of five minutes. Part way through the pre-service portion of the
pilot, Durham decided to stop having intake workers administer consents. Instead, the caseworkers were merely required to hand clients a letter that ex-
plained the project and said that they would be contacted by an interviewer.
Exhibit 10 shows the letter used in Durham. Alternatively, a similar statement could be included in the routine application forms, with the statement

EXHIBIT 9

ILLUSTRATIVE CONSENT FORM

---

_____ COUNTY DEPARTMENT OF SOCIAL SERVICES

In order to learn more about the effectiveness of _____ County's social services, we would like to ask some questions about how things are going for you. Through the project we hope to identify improvements needed in our service system.

Taking part in these interviews is completely voluntary. No one has to take part in this project unless they want to. One interview will be done within a few days, and one about 8-9 months later.

The information given will remain confidential; only information on groups of clients will be shown in any reports.

---

I have read or listened to the above information regarding the interviews, and I am willing to co-operate in the interviews.

This consent is valid until: _____
                            (No longer than 1 year from date below)

Signature: _____ Date: _____

RELATIONSHIP TO PRIMARY RECIPIENT: _____

Please list two people who will probably know how to reach you in the event you move before the second interview.

Name: _____ Tel.: _____

Address: _____

Name: _____ Tel.: _____

Address: _____

EXHIBIT 10

LETTER GIVEN TO CLIENTS BY CASEWORKERS
IN DURHAM COUNTY PILOT TEST

## County of Durham
### Department of Social Services

DANIEL C. HUDGINS
DIRECTOR

P. O. BOX 810
DURHAM, NORTH CAROLINA 27702

    The Durham County Department of Social Services is studying ways to improve their services to clients.  In order to do this, some clients are being asked to participate in "before and  after" interviews.  You may be contacted within a few days by one of the interviewers.  If you agree to participate, you will have a short interview then and another one in a few months.  Both interviews will ask about how you are doing in your day-to-day life.  In the second interview you'll also have a chance to say what you thought of the services you received and give suggestions for how they can be improved.

    The information from the interviews will not affect your eligibility for services.  You are not required to participate.  However, we hope you will, because the more clients who give information, the more we'll learn about how the services affect clients and how services can be improved.

that receipt of services is not contingent upon consent. After this procedure was started (late in the Durham pilot test), nine clients were referred for monitoring. Of these, seven consented when contacted by the interviewer, and two could not be located for consent and interview. There were no refusals. It is possible that the information letter may have contributed to client willingness to participate, but the numbers are too small to permit a conclusion.

As shown earlier, the overall refusal rate in Chesapeake was 18 percent (11 percent refused initially, 1 percent consented initially but refused at the time of the pre-service interview, and 6 percent consented initially, completed the pre-service interview, but refused the follow-up interview). In Durham, the total refusal rate was also 18 percent (16 percent refused initially, 1 percent at the time of the pre-service interview, and 1 percent at follow up). These refusal rates are not too bad but still are higher than desirable. The reasons for the refusals are not clear. (Because of reservations of agency staff about "pushing" clients, clients were not asked about their reasons for refusing.) But ways should be sought to reduce refusal rates. Consent rates might improve if written consents were not required. The increased formality of written consents may create some anxiety in clients. It also seems that if consents were routinized as part of the regular application process, there would be fewer refusals. An information letter like the one used in Durham might also help. Whatever steps are taken to improve consent rates, however, agencies must take care not to shortcut the clients' rights to informed consent or refusal.

Recommendation. An agency should obtain a legal position on the necessity for written consents. It should provide its legal office with information such as that presented in this chapter to assure that the no-written-consent-is-required possibility is adequately considered. (It is tempting for legal staff to take the easy way out and, for complete safety's sake, call for written consents.)

If an agency finds that written consent is required, we recommend one of the following three approaches: (1) Incorporate written consent into the application process. A consent form could be added to any other forms, such as collateral consent forms, which clients sign at the time of application.[1] This has the drawback that if these forms are completed during intake interviews, intake workers may have to spend additional time with clients. (2) Have interviewers see clients for consents and interviews immediately after their intake sessions. This requires that an interviewer be available at such

---

1. In Chesapeake, in order to receive services each client must sign a confidentiality form unless the client is physically or mentally unable to do so. The Commonwealth of Virginia Privacy Protection law requires that a person sign this consent form before social services can make collateral contacts to determine the client's eligibility for services. If the client does not apply in person, this form is mailed or brought to the client. It was suggested that the monitoring consent form be stapled to this or, preferably, that a few lines be added to the bottom of the form to legally cover the interviews. Since many clients were likely to sign without understanding what they had signed, the interviewers would need to be trained to explain the project and get verbal permission before starting the interview.

times and that the client spend additional time in the agency office. In spite of these drawbacks the Chesapeake working group strongly recommends this latter method. Only in cases where there is no in-person application do they recommend the third approach. (3) <u>At a later date, have interviewers obtain written consent and do interviews at the same time</u>. This approach requires that interviews be conducted in person in the client's home or that clients be asked to come into the office. This method was used in Chesapeake when intake workers failed to ask clients to sign consents at time of application. However, since it was more costly and refusal rates were higher than when consent was obtained at intake, Chesapeake thought this method the least desirable of the three. In Durham County, however, this approach seems to have worked well.


## Confidentiality

Once the client consents and is interviewed, procedures to safeguard the confidentiality of the information must be followed. In general, names and other information traceable to an individual client such as address and telephone number should be removed from the questionnaire as soon as the interview process (including any verifications that the interviewing supervisor deems necessary) is completed, leaving only a code number. The coordinator should probably be the only person with access to the list which identifies code numbers with individual clients.

One deviation from this general rule is that the intake interview information on individual clients perhaps should be made available to caseworkers for their use in assessing client needs. As will be discussed further in Chapter 5, pre-service information may be useful to caseworkers, especially in agencies where intake interviews do not include full psychosocial assessments. An agency might also decide to provide follow-up information to caseworkers. If so, the clients should be explicitly told that this will be done. However, individual client satisfaction information should <u>not</u> be given to clients' caseworkers. This could affect the frankness of client responses. The agency has an obligation to inform the client about what interview information will be seen by whom.

Besides the coordinator and possibly caseworkers or their supervisors, no one in the agency should have access to interview information identified with individual clients.

Finally, the reports prepared showing the outcome findings should show grouped data and not data on individual clients or data that in any way would permit others to identify individual clients.

# CHAPTER 4.

# IMPLEMENTATION AND COST OF OUTCOME
# MONITORING PROCEDURES

Two different levels of implementation are discussed here: (1) for individual local social services agencies, and (2) for state governments that seek to monitor outcomes across a number of local agencies. Most of the start-up and ongoing coordination steps described in this chapter apply to both levels of government and to a wide range of outcome monitoring procedures.

## Steps Involved in Starting These
## Outcome Monitoring Procedures

1. <u>Secure top management support</u>. This is vital, and without it an agency might as well not bother to attempt to monitor outcomes. Management should consider the potential uses for the information provided by the procedures (see Chapter 5) and how much the information will cost (as discussed later in this chapter). A commitment should be made for at least a one-year trial, and preferably two years, since the first year includes several months of procedure-development work.

2. <u>Convey clearly to staff top management's commitment to monitoring client outcomes</u>. Lack of sufficient attention to this step caused some early problems in the pilot test agencies.

3. <u>As soon as possible, select a high-level agency manager to direct the overall effort</u>. This person should be someone who is interested in and will be supportive of the effort.

4. <u>Convene a "working group."</u> Include administrative and supervisory representatives and preferably some service staff caseworkers. If the agency has a client participation program, a client might also be included in the working group. This working group will be responsible for designing and testing the procedures and for getting the tested procedures started. The lack of a working group in one pilot test agency was seen as a major cause of a breakdown in the outcome monitoring procedures.

In addition to designing, testing, and initiating the procedures, the working group should be responsible for keeping the rest of agency staff informed about the procedures. This task can be handled both informally and formally by such means as distributing periodic progress reports and copies of data collection forms. Issues that might be controversial--such as the procedure for determining which protective services clients should be included in the monitoring sample--should be discussed with the staff members concerned.

The working group will need to meet frequently--perhaps weekly--during the first few months of the initial year and monthly thereafter.

Agencies that lack in-house technical capability for measurement and sampling design should consider seeking outside technical assistance for their working groups.

5. Designate a "coordinator." The coordinator will be responsible for day-to-day management of the procedures. The coordinator should be able to put a substantial amount of time into the work. In a local effort, up to half of one person's time may be required, while a full-time person is required to coordinate a statewide effort.[1] In addition, experiences in the pilot tests indicate that an assistant coordinator is required for back-up.

The primary local coordinators in the three test sites were members of agency professional staffs--in Chesapeake, a caseworker who carried a small caseload and handled "special projects"; in Stanly County, the case management and supportive services supervisor; and in Durham County, the director of the adult services division. In Chesapeake, the coordinator handled most of the work himself, with some clerical assistance and a back-up coordinator who filled in when the coordinator was assigned to an out-of-town project. In Stanly and Durham, however, the local coordinators assigned to the project had numerous other responsibilities, and so the state coordinator handled much of the coordination in one of the two counties. In the other county, since the state did not coordinate and the local coordinator was committed to other tasks, there were difficulties in coordination. (See the discussion later in the chapter of various possible ways of dividing state and local roles.) Judging from the pilot test experiences, it seems that while a local coordinator should be a member of the administrative or professional staff with some experience and authority, and preferably some analytic background, the coordinator need not be a top administrator. The coordinator should be someone, like the co-ordinator in the Chesapeake test, who has considerable time to devote to the day-to-day running of outcome monitoring. We estimate that coordination will take one-third to one-half of the coordinator's time; few high-level adminis-trative staff can devote that amount of time to a single activity. In a smaller agency like Stanly County's, however, which does not have any casework staff assigned to full-time special projects, it may be appropriate to have a supervisor handle the project.

The assistant coordinator should be someone who can understand the pro-cedures thoroughly enough to assure that the system can continue when the pri-mary coordinator is absent. Since there is considerable routine paperwork

_____

1. The coordinator in Chesapeake spent approximately 30 percent of his time on the outcome monitoring work during the six months (August-October 1977, and May-July 1978) during which the intake and follow-up interviews were being conducted, record data collected, and data edited and keypunched. This does not count time spent by the coordinator in the working group's procedure design efforts. Since the coordinator's work did not include analysis of the data, which would normally be part of the coordinator's role, we prefer to use the more conservative estimate of 50 percent for the time required from the coordinator once the procedures are designed and started.

involved in managing the ongoing procedures, the coordinator might wish to have a secretary as assistant coordinator. In the Durham County pilot test, an administrative secretary satisfactorily handled the assignment of interviews and the record-keeping logs that were used to keep track of client referrals and disposition.

There are certain to be issues that the coordinator cannot resolve alone. The continued participation of the working group in the system is important. There should be regular working group meetings to review how the monitoring is going. In addition, the coordinator should be able to convene special meetings when problems arise between the regular meetings.

We stress the importance of the coordinator, assistant coordinator, and working group in the success of a monitoring system. In one of the three pilot test sites, the coordinator, the back-up coordinator, and the working group had conflicting demands on their time, and when the coordinator became unable to work on monitoring due to conflicting demands on her time, the interviewing stopped completely; cases did not get referred or assigned to interviewers. Problems such as this are bound to arise, and if they are not caught quickly, the quality of the outcome data can be seriously damaged and the process can even stop altogether.

The role of the coordinator and the tasks involved in coordination are discussed in more detail in the next section.

6. Decide what data should be collected. Determine what questions should be included in the client interview questionnaires and record information forms. Chapter 2, the illustrative questionnaire contained in Appendix 1, and the detailed discussion of the questionnaire contained in Appendix 2 can be used as a starting point. An agency might find that the illustrative questionnaire fits its needs without major modification, but the process of examining the questionnaire is a good way for the working group to begin thinking about outcomes and about the information collected by the procedures.

One good mechanism for examining the questionnaire and record information forms is to consider in detail a group of past or current case records, checking to see if the clients' problems and the objectives of services in these cases are adequately covered in the questionnaire and record forms. The Chesapeake pilot test working group, working in teams of two with Institute project staff, examined about fifty case records, in an intensive two-day effort. Both the working group and the Institute staff considered this exercise extremely valuable. It familiarized everyone with the questionnaire and uncovered issues whose resolution improved the questionnaire.

7. Decide upon procedures for selecting clients for monitoring and for administering interviews. Chapter 3 outlines the issues involved in these procedures and can serve as a starting point for the working group on this step.

8. Select and train interviewers. A number of specific suggestions are provided in Chapter 3.

9. <u>Pretest the pre-service and follow-up questionnaires</u>. Use a small sample of clients and modify questionnaire structure and wording as needed. The pretest is a vital part of implementing outcome monitoring procedures. It attempts to resolve the following issues: (1) Are the proposed modes of interviewing (telephone, in-person at home, in-person at the office) feasible options for the clients of the agency? (2) Are the interviewers sufficiently capable and well trained? (3) How long does an average interview take? (4) Is the questionnaire comprehensible to the respondents? Are there questions which should be altered, dropped, or added? (5) Are the introductory remarks appropriate, and are the skip instructions clear? (6) Are there any problems in the procedures for informing clients and obtaining consent?

Pretesting the questionnaire is an excellent way to get the interviewers involved, which is important since the success of monitoring depends largely on their efforts. Interviewers should be asked to report on questions that were difficult or awkward to administer, problems with skip patterns and difficulties encountered in locating respondents, obtaining consents, or conducting interviews. After a pretest is completed, the working group should meet with the interviewers to discuss and resolve the issues raised by the interviewers. Incorporating interviewer suggestions helps interviewers feel the project is theirs and not something thrust upon them. In any case, interviewers are often the ones most familiar with difficulties in the administration of the questionnaire. In the pilot tests, interviewers made significant contributions to improvement of the questionnaires.

Following the pretest, the questionnaires and interviewing procedures should be revised as needed and the interviewers retrained to the new procedures.

10. <u>Set up a "logging" system</u>. This permits tracking of the procedural steps for each monitoring client. This log should include dates of application for service, assignment of pre-service interview, completion of pre-service interview, and so on. See Exhibit 11 for an example of a "log" form. We also suggest using a second log to permit all persons involved in the monitoring effort to keep track of their time required during the pilot year so that estimates of annual costs can be made.

11. <u>Implement the procedures for the pilot year</u>. Start selecting clients as they come through intake, giving them pre-service interviews and, later, follow-up interviews. After perhaps two to three months of intakes have been completed, stop client selection and pre-service interviews temporarily, and review thoroughly the procedures and the data obtained. Interviewers and the staff who are responsible for selecting clients and managing and logging the interview procedures should meet with the working group to discuss any problems that have been found. When these have been resolved and it appears that the process is proceeding reasonably smoothly, resume intake interviewing of new clients.

12. <u>Establish procedures for effective reporting of the outcome data</u>. This includes design of summary data formats, based on identification of the various aggregations of outcomes that are most useful--such as by type of client, by type of problem, by type of service provided, by amount of service provided, by geographical location--see Chapter 5. The working group, as part

## EXHIBIT 11

## OUTCOME MONITORING COORDINATOR'S LOG[1]

| Client Code # | Name of Primary Client and Agency Case Number | Name of Person to Be Interviewed and Relationship to Client | Date Client Applied for Service | Date Pre-Service Interview Assigned; Interviewer | Date Pre-Service Interview Completed or Dropped | Final Status of Pre-Service Interview (completed, refused, unable to find, etc.) and Comments | Date Follow-Up Interview Assigned; Interviewer | Date Follow-Up Interview Completed or Dropped | Final Status of Follow-Up Interview (completed, refused, unable to find, etc.) and Comments |
|---|---|---|---|---|---|---|---|---|---|
| 0001 | | | | | | | | | |
| 0002 | | | | | | | | | |
| 0003 | | | | | | | | | |
| 0004 | | | | | | | | | |
| 0005 | | | | | | | | | |
| 0006 | | | | | | | | | |
| 0007 | | | | | | | | | |
| 0008 | | | | | | | | | |
| 0009 | | | | | | | | | |
| 0010 | | | | | | | | | |

1. In the pilot tests, logs also included time spent by the coordinators and interviewers on various tasks. An agency might want to collect such data for purposes of estimating the "costs" of monitoring.

of this task, should select a "scoring" procedure to combine, for each outcome dimension, the findings from a number of data elements.[1]  A "mechanical" procedure should be developed so that outcome scores can be calculated by clerical staff, or, if possible, by using automatic data-processing equipment.[2]

To assure that the scoring, analysis, and reporting procedures will provide data which will be most useful to managers, we suggest that the working group solicit the opinions of a variety of supervisors and managers regarding what types of data and level of detail they need for various program and policy decisions.

13.  At the end of the pilot test year, the findings from the test should be reviewed.  The cost of the procedures should be compared with the potential usefulness of the data.  If outcome monitoring is to be continued, the procedures should be reviewed and modifications made as necessary.  The procedures then should be "institutionalized" as a regular activity of the agency, parallel to procedures for the collection of expenditure and service activity data.  Reports summarizing client outcome findings preferably should be coordinated with cost and service activity reports and be made available jointly for budgeting and other decisionmaking activities.

Periodic review--at least annual--of the outcome procedures and data is desirable to assure that the data continue to be satisfactory, that unneeded tasks and data are deleted, and that the usefulness of the information continues to be worth the cost.

## Steps in Coordinating Ongoing Procedures

The coordinator, with help from the assistant coordinator and clerical staff, will perform a number of tasks required to maintain the outcome monitoring procedures once they are implemented, both in the pilot year and in subsequent years.  The coordinator is responsible for seeing that the procedures run smoothly.  The pilot tests showed that without steady attention from a coordinator, the procedures will quickly flounder.  Coordination involves the following tasks:

1.  Obtain, on a daily or weekly basis, case records or face sheets for all new clients.

2.  Decide which member of each client family group is considered the "primary client" for monitoring purposes and which member is to be interviewed.  (See Chapter 3.)

---

1.  An illustrative scoring procedure is described in Appendix 1.

2.  Computer scoring and analysis of the data can save much manual labor and is needed for large agencies or statewide monitoring.  Agencies with small samples of clients will likely find hand scoring and analysis to be appropriate.  The participation of a staff member who "likes to play with numbers" can greatly enhance the ability of the agency to get the most information out of the data.

3.  Enter each new monitoring case on a log (see Exhibit 11) with an assigned monitoring number.

4.  Check logs daily or weekly to see which clients are due for follow-up interviews.  Order case records and check for current addresses and changes in client condition or living arrangements that may affect the choice of who should be interviewed.  (For example, if a child had changed foster homes, one might interview a different foster mother; if an aged client had deteriorated badly it might be necessary to interview a family member rather than the client.)

5.  Assign cases to interviewers and fill out interviewer information forms, with information on how to contact clients and whatever background information is to be provided to interviewers.

6.  Collect completed (or failed) interview questionnaires from interviewers and record on log.

7.  Review and edit questionnaires as they are received.  The coordinator should check to see that responses are consistent with each other and that skip instructions have been followed properly.  If the questionnaires will be keypunched, the coordinator will have to insert some codes, such as for "missing" or "don't know" responses, and code items that were not precoded for interviewers.  It is preferable that the coordinator review the forms as they come in.  The review should not only be the first step in preparing the data for analysis, but also should serve as a quality check on interviews and as a clue to needs for further training on items where interviewers have problems.  When errors are detected, the coordinator can go back to the interviewers and help them to correct the problems.

8.  Collect required information from records.

9.  Calculate the scores for each client from the questionnaire and record data--pre-service scores, follow-up scores, and "change" scores.  If an agency is using a computer for analysis, the scores can either be generated by the computer from keypunched questionnaires and record data or be done by hand and then keypunched for use in the analysis.

10.  Have the data that will be used in the analysis keypunched or tabulated.  If possible, all data that will be used in analysis should be keypunched.  Even if an agency lacks the hardware or programming capability to perform analyses entirely by computer, it should probably keypunch the data if it has keypunch, card-sorting, and print-out equipment.  Keypunching the data onto cards facilitates hand analysis, because it allows for different "sortings" of cards for different analyses, whereas hand tabulations done in one format for one analysis may be inconvenient in format for a different analysis.  Retabulating by hand is more time-consuming than card sorting with an automatic cardsorter.

In all cases, we suggest that a run out of the data be obtained and formulated so that responses for each client are readily readable.  These sheets can be used to check data, to manually examine patterns of responses for any client, and to permit manual tabulations and other analyses when computer assistance is not available in a timely way.

Which outcome data should be keypunched: all of the individual question responses or only the summary module "scores"? The answer to this question depends upon the available computer capability and the uses that will be made of the data. For many purposes, the summary scores will be sufficient. Occasionally, though, an agency might want to analyze responses to some specific questions; then these questions should be keypunched in addition to the scores and indicators.

11. If the agency does not contract out the interviewing, the coordinator may also be involved in recruiting, training, and supervising interviewers and, if so, should plan to meet regularly with them. The coordinator will be in a good position to detect and remedy problems in interviewing quality or other problems in the procedures.

12. The coordinator also should be responsible for the maintenance of confidentiality--separating client names from client interview data and making sure that interviewers respect clients' privacy and do not discuss interviews with anyone in the agency besides the coordinator. In some cases clients may request that interviewers report problems to the agency, or interviewers may be worried about clients who seem to them to be in urgent need. Interviewers should discuss such cases with the coordinator, and the coordinator should exercise careful judgment in deciding what action to take.

13. At regular intervals--annually, semi-annually, or quarterly, depending on the uses that are to be made of the data--the coordinator, with clerical or automatic data-processing assistance, should analyze the data from all cases that have had follow-up interviews since the last analysis point, and provide reports on the results.

If possible, the data should be analyzed using a computer. However, some agencies may lack the necessary hardware or programming capability. Two alternatives to full computer processing are (1) keypunching the data onto cards and using a cardsorter and printer to aid with cross-tabulations, with other tasks such as scoring individual questionnaires done manually, or (2) tabulating the data entirely by hand.

Data from large statewide samples should be computer-analyzed, and state-level agencies will usually have the computer capability for this. Most analyses required for local agencies with comparatively small samples can be accomplished using keypunched data, a cardsorter, a printer, and a small calculator. Doing tabulations and analysis entirely by hand is arduous and time-consuming and will limit the quantity of analysis undertaken. Nevertheless, it is still possible to do some useful analyses entirely by hand.

If an agency decides to do computer analysis, outcome data can be handled by using prepackaged programs for analysis and transferring the resulting information by hand to display tables. An alternative is to use a computer program to generate the form directly from the data.[1]

---

1. The Urban Institute has developed a computer program to display a number of cross-tabulations for any given question on the same sheet, e.g.,

(continued)

## Options for a Statewide System

There are a number of options that state level agencies can consider. These include the following:

1.  Obtain data on client outcomes from a sample of local agency clients throughout the state, with the procedures being operated by the state agency.

2.  Obtain annual client outcome data statewide, but rely on individual local agencies to operate the procedures.

3.  Do not attempt to obtain statewide data, but encourage, and provide support for, individual or local agencies to introduce the client outcome monitoring procedures to provide data mainly for local agency use.

Some of the implications of each of these options are discussed in the following paragraphs.

1.  <u>Statewide samples, with state central staff operating the procedures.</u> The central office would be responsible for the initial development of the procedures, and would handle the pre-service and follow-up interviews, using interviewers recruited and paid for by the central office. Data analysis and reporting would be handled centrally. A local liaison would screen all cases at intake and provide the central office with lists of clients for monitoring. Data from agency records could either be provided by the local liaisons or be obtained by staff sent out from the central office. The local role, both in design and in the ongoing work, would not be large. Particularly for small local agencies that cannot commit large amounts of staff time to questionnaire and procedure design and testing, the state should be prepared with a well-developed package of questionnaires and procedures. We urge, however, that the state utilize local agency personnel in at least an advisory role.

This "centralized" option will be easier and more appropriate for states with state-administered services. In states with locally administered services, this option would require substantial cooperation from the local agencies. The legal and ethical issues related to confidentiality would need to be worked out clearly to alleviate local concerns about the provision of client names and addresses and other information to the state central office. Special care must be taken to maintain client confidentiality.

It is very important that the state coordinator and the local agency staff be clear as to the division of labor. For instance, the local role

_____

(continued)
to display client satisfaction tabulated against age group, sex, problem type, and service, on the same page. This greatly reduces the paper that users have to look at and facilitates making comparisons across such groupings. Documentation on the program as well as a tape copy can be obtained from The Urban Institute Computer Services Division: J. Gueron and B. Ouyang, "UI-MCTAB: A Multiple Crosstab Program" (Washington, D.C.: The Urban Institute, 1974).

might be limited entirely to referring cases and collecting data from case records, with the state handling assignment and supervision of interviewers. If the state wanted the local staff to play a larger role, this should be discussed in advance and agreement reached on exactly where the local role begins and ends (allowing, of course, for later renegotiation of roles if the initial ones do not work out well).

A key issue is the coverage by the state of numerous local agencies (for example, 100 in North Carolina and 116 in Virginia). For example, if a state has 70 local agencies, obtaining outcomes on only 100 clients per agency would require obtaining pre-service and follow-up interviews from 7,000 clients, a costly endeavor. A more viable strategy is one in which the largest 5 to 10 agencies in the state are sampled, with additional samples for the remainder of each major region of the state. As noted in Chapter 3, the few largest agencies often account for a substantial proportion of total expenditures. In Virginia, for example, the largest 10 of the 116 local agencies account for nearly 50 percent of annual Title XX expenditures.

2. <u>Statewide samples, with local agencies operating the procedures</u>. In this option the local agencies would have a larger role in designing the data-collection procedures. The state, however, must place some constraints on local variations of the procedures to assure that data will be comparable across a number of agencies. Obtaining local agencies' agreement to a more or less common set of procedures could be quite difficult, and ample time is necessary for this process. Once the procedures are implemented, the state should play an active role in maintaining the quality and comparability of the data from local agencies.

Since this option involves a state-mandated effort, <u>the state should provide funds to local agencies to help operate the procedures</u>. The state should support the cost of interviewing and should also consider helping agencies obtain interviewers, possibly through a central state contract system. Local difficulties in obtaining, training, and maintaining interviewers were a major problem in our pilot test sites.

3. <u>Encouragement, and financial and technical support, to local agencies to undertake client outcome monitoring primarily for local uses</u>. In this option, the state does not attempt to obtain a statewide sample of clients, thus limiting the usefulness of the outcome data for statewide program or policy decisions (although it still might use local outcome data for certain limited issues). The emphasis is on helping individual local agencies improve their own program and policy decisionmaking efforts. <u>For this third option to be meaningful, it should involve substantial financial and technical assistance to local agencies</u>. Although Chesapeake undertook the pilot test on its own initiative, without financial support from the state, developed an active working group and coordinator, and provided its own interviewers, The Urban Institute was heavily involved, and it seems likely that most comparable local agencies would require considerable technical assistance to implement outcome monitoring procedures. Moreover, the burden of providing interviewers will be quite difficult for most local agencies to sustain. Assigning several clerical staff to monitoring entailed some sacrifice for Chesapeake; and Stanly and Durham Counties found that they were unable, without help, to maintain local interviewers.

We believe that each state should at the very least exercise this third option, even if the state does not choose to go forward with the more ambitious options in (1) and (2). This option can also be used as a first-phase effort that may lead to option (2).

## Cost of the Outcome Monitoring System

The discussion of costs is split into two portions: (1) ongoing costs after the initial implementation work is completed--for local agencies and for statewide monitoring, and (2) one-time start-up costs involved in the initial modification and implementation of the procedures.

### Ongoing Costs: Local Agency

We estimate that an ongoing monitoring system in a local agency with an average intake of 100 clients per month would require about 2-3/4 to 3-1/2 employee-years of effort annually (about forty thousand to fifty thousand dollars), assuming that the agency sought to monitor all incoming clients.[1] This includes the cost of coordinating and conducting pre-service and follow-up interviews with these clients, obtaining some data from client records, keypunching the data, and doing some basic data analysis. Exhibit 12 shows how these costs were calculated based on the pilot test data. The amount of actual out-of-pocket costs will depend on whether existing resources are available to undertake some of these activities.

A cost of forty thousand to fifty thousand dollars may seem high, but it is a small fraction of the annual budget for the average public social service agency. Without this much effort, it does not seem likely that an agency can obtain this type of detailed client-outcome information. Other procedures, particularly those involving caseworkers evaluating their own clients' outcomes, may appear to cost less because they involve no out-of-pocket costs, but they use costly caseworker time and may produce data of questionable usefulness, as discussed in Chapter 2. Some of the work of the outcome monitoring procedures recommended here may be handled without out-of-pocket costs, if an agency has some staff who can help with the procedures. For example, in the pilot test, Chesapeake used its own staff for coordinating and interviewing activities and therefore incurred "out-of-pocket" costs only for such items as travel, paper, and telephone. Although using current staff may be feasible in some agencies, it still involves "opportunity cost"--these staff members will not be able to do other things they might have done if they were not doing outcome monitoring work. Therefore, our estimates include all costs, regardless of whether agencies will actually lay out additional money for interviewing and coordinating staff.

---

1. The pilot tests themselves required minimal "out-of-pocket" costs; the agencies used existing staff. However, these tests covered intakes for only three months.

EXHIBIT 12

ESTIMATED ANNUAL COST FOR OUTCOME MONITORING
IN A LOCAL SOCIAL SERVICE AGENCY

| Cost Element | Estimated Staff Time in Employee Years[1] | Estimated Dollar Cost[1] |
|---|---|---|
| 1.  Interviewers' time | 1-3/4 – 2-1/3 years | $19,700 – 26,200 |
| 2.  Coordinator's time | 1/3 – 1/2 year | 7,500 – 11,250 |
| 3.  Working group time | 1/6 year | 3,800 |
| 4.  Clerical assistance | 1/2 year | 5,600 |
| 5.  Telephone | | 360 |
| 6.  Transportation | | 800 |
| 7.  Paper and duplication | | 1,500 |
| 8.  Data-processing cost (machine costs) | | 1,000 |
| Total | 2-3/4 – 3-1/2 years | $40,260 – 50,510 |

1.  See the following for explanatory notes for each cost element.  These costs will not necessarily all be out-of-pocket costs.  The amount of actual out-of-pocket costs required will depend on the extent to which existing resources can be used to undertake this work.

Assumptions Behind Local Cost Estimates

Item 1.  Interviewers.  These figures are for an agency that has about 100 clients per month who are selected for monitoring.  With attrition comparable to that in the pilot tests, this would mean that about 840 pre-service interviews would be completed (70 percent of 1,200) and about 720 follow-up interviews would be completed (60 percent of 1,200).  (See Chapter 3.)  If each interviewer averaged 4 completed interviews per day, 19 working days a month, then slightly less than 1-3/4 person-years would be required.  If each interviewer averaged 3 completed interviews per day, then slightly less than 2-1/3 person-years would be required.  (See Chapter 3 for discussion of how the 3 to 4 interviews per day standard was derived.  This standard allows for supervision time with the coordinator, and other time not directly spent in interviewing.)  The salary figure used was $9,000 basic annual salary plus 25 percent fringe benefits for a clerical employee, for a total of $11,250.

EXHIBIT 12 (Continued)

Item 2. Coordinator. This figure is based on the Chesapeake coordinator's logs of time spent on the project during the 3 months of pre-service interviews and 3 months of follow-up interviews and analysis. The coordinator's salary is figured on a base of $18,000 annual salary, plus 25 percent fringes, for a total of $22,500. This estimate of cost for the coordinator's time includes the cost of analytic work and assumes that the coordinator, with the help of the working group, can provide in-house analytic capability. If this is not the case, the cost of a part-time analyst or consultant should be added.

Item 3. Working group. The basis for this estimate is that a working group of 6 professional and managerial staff would meet one-half day per month, for oversight of the project, with base salary similar to the coordinator's.

Item 4. Clerical assistance. Although the Chesapeake coordinator did most of the work, except keypunching, without clerical assistance, we include this figure because we believe such assistance will usually be necessary, particularly during analysis of the data and writing of reports.

Item 5. Telephone. A local agency might not incur any additional out-of-pocket costs for telephone calls made locally, but we included a telephone company estimate of the annual cost of an additional telephone line, in order to be on the conservative side.

Item 6. Transportation. Based on the pilot tests, our assumption is that 60 percent of the interviews can be done by telephone, provided either that written consents are not required or that they are obtained as a routine part of intake applications and do not necessitate trips to clients' homes (see Chapter 3). An additional 10 percent might be done at the agency offices, leaving 30 percent to be done at clients' homes, with travel costs figures at 17¢ per mile, for 470 round trips with a somewhat arbitrary average of 10 miles per round trip.

Item 7. Paper and duplication costs. These were figured at 3¢ a copy for 1,600 copies of questionnaires at 25 pages each, plus miscellaneous logs, reports, and other papers.

## Ongoing Costs:  Statewide

The cost of state monitoring efforts will vary according to which of the
options discussed under "Options for a Statewide System" is chosen by the
state.  If the second or third options are used, the costs per local monitoring site will be comparable to those given for a local agency, except that in
option 2 each local agency might monitor fewer clients, thus reducing the cost
of interviewing, and they might send the data to the state for analysis.  For
options 2 and 3, cost sharing between the state and local agencies would occur.

If the first option is used, with the work centralized in a state evaluation office, a state should be prepared for ongoing costs of $150,000-$180,000
annually (approximately 10-1/2 to 14 employee-years if all work is done in-
house) for pre-service and follow-up data on three thousand clients.  Exhibit 13 shows how this figure is calculated.

The estimates do not include the time it takes to set up the procedures
and train liaison persons in each local agency to refer clients for interviewing, nor does it include the time spent by these local liaisons.  A sample
size of 3,000 permits the state to make some limited comparisons among perhaps
fifteen areas of the state (averaging about 200 clients each)--perhaps seven
of the largest county agencies with the remaining agencies grouped into eight
regions.  This sample size of 3,000 clients is not sufficient to provide reliable outcome data for each local agency in most states, although in some
small states it might be adequate.  If a state wished to have a large enough
sample to provide data reliable at the local level for breakouts of, say, four
client or service groups for, say, twenty-five county agencies, it would be
required to have a statewide sample of around 10,000 clients (or more than
20,000 interviews), which would drive the cost of interviewing up to over
$200,000.

## Start-up Costs

The cost estimates just given represent ongoing costs, not start-up
costs.  In the first year, questionnaire revision, adaptation of the procedures to fit the agency, and training will take considerable costly professional time.  The pilot test experience, because it involved basic exploration and development, much of which should not have to be repeated, did not
provide a good basis for estimating the start-up costs for an agency starting
from where the pilot tests left off.  However, there are a few major special
start-up costs that are roughly identifiable:

- Several days of the time of top managers in the agency are needed
  to consider client outcome data needs and to identify the decisionmaking uses to which the outcome data will be put.

- A working group will need to meet frequently during implementation.
  As discussed earlier, it should include a high-level manager and
  several other managers, supervisors, and a caseworker or analyst who
  will be the coordinator.  Weekly half-day meetings over a period of
  three months for six professional staff would not be an unreasonable
  estimate of the time needed for the initial work of adapting the procedures and questionnaires to the special needs of the agency.

EXHIBIT 13

ESTIMATE OF ANNUAL COST FOR OUTCOME MONITORING IN A STATE
SOCIAL SERVICE AGENCY USING CENTRAL STATE
STAFF TO ADMINISTER THE PROCEDURES

| Cost Element | Estimated Staff Time in Employee Years[1] | Estimated Dollar Cost[1] |
|---|---|---|
| 1. Interviewers' time | 7 - 10 years | $65,000 - 78,000 |
| 2. Coordinator/analysts' time | 1-1/3 - 2 years | 33,250 - 50,000 |
| 3. State working group time | 1/6 year | 4,200 |
| 4. Clerical assistance | 2 years | 25,000 |
| 5. Telephone | | 5,000 |
| 6. Transportation | | 5,000 |
| 7. Paper and duplication | | 6,000 |
| 8. Data-processing costs (machine costs) | | 4,000 |
| Total | 10-1/2 - 14-1/6 years | $147,450 - 177,200 |

1. See the following for explanatory notes for each cost element. These costs will not necessarily all be out-of-pocket costs. The amount of actual out-of-pocket expenditures required will depend on the extent to which existing resources can be used to undertake this work.

Assumptions Behind State Cost Estimates

1. Item 1. Interviewers. This figure is calculated on the basis of $10-$12 per completed interview. Allowing for nonconsents and other sources of attrition from the sample, 6,500 interviews are likely to be required to obtain a total of 3,000 clients with complete pre-service and follow-up data. If the state uses government employees for the interviewing, approximately 7 to 10 persons are likely to be required, or the state could contract with survey firms for interviews.

EXHIBIT 13 (continued)

Item 2. Coordinator/analysts' time. Without assuming either "econ- omies of scale" or additional efforts due to being a centralized state effort, this figure was calculated by multiplying the local coordinator's time by 4, since there would be approximately 4 times as many interviews. Like the other figures, these do not take into account start-up costs, which would involve many on-site visits to local agencies. These figures assume that once a sys- tem is ongoing, only occasional trips to local agencies should be required. The salary figures are $20,000, plus 25 percent fringe benefits, for a total of $25,000. The state coordinators should have analytic experience.

Item 3. Working group. Calculated on the same basis as for local agen- cies, except using the higher professional salary cited in Item 2.

Item 4. Clerical assistance. As with the coordinators' time, clerical time is the local agency clerical time estimate multiplied by 4, but with the salary figure at a base of $10,000 per year, plus 25 percent for fringe bene- fits, for a total of $12,500.

Item 5. Telephone. For a statewide sample of 3,000 clients, no single locality would be likely to require an extra telephone line for interviewing. However, a considerable amount of statewide telephoning would be required for coordination, and therefore the costs of area WATS lines are included. If interviews can be done locally, cost will be less; if they are all done from a central office and a statewide WATS line is used, costs will be consider- ably higher. If interviewers call from their own homes rather than from lo- cal agency offices, and they are reimbursed for telephone costs, the figure for telephone costs will be higher.

Item 6. Transportation. Costs are based on having locally based inter- viewers travel to clients' homes for 30 percent of all interviews, 10 miles round trip, 17¢ per mile (with the other 70 percent being done either by telephone or at the agency offices). In addition, the cost of travel around the state for the coordinator was estimated at an additional $1,700 per year.

Item 7. Paper and duplication costs. These were figured at 3¢ a copy for 6,500 copies of questionnaires at 25 pages each, plus miscellaneous logs, reports, and other papers.

- Initial training of the interviewers would involve a one-day session for discussion and role play, plus several later meetings to discuss pre-test and later experiences with the questionnaire. Ongoing supervision is necessary, but is included in the costs of ongoing coordination that were estimated above.

- We strongly advise that technical assistance be provided during initial implementation and to a lesser extent during ongoing work. This might be obtained from a state university school of social work or survey research laboratory. The cost of such assistance is difficult to estimate.

- An all-staff meeting should be held to introduce agency staff to the monitoring procedures and the potential uses for the data, and to get staff input.

- The conduct and analysis of the pretest will probably require a solid month of the coordinator's time, above the time spent by the working group as a whole during initial implementation.

While these costs for initial implementation can be substantial, they will be at least somewhat offset by the fact that fewer interviews will be done during the first-year trial phase, and thus, there will be savings on interviewing and travel costs. Because these initial costs involve little interviewing, they do not require large out-of-pocket outlays (except possibly for technical assistance), but instead involve "opportunity costs" in the professional time that is taken away from other activities.

# CHAPTER 5.

# PRESENTATION AND USE OF OUTCOME DATA

Social service officials have seldom obtained outcome information on a regular basis. The pilot tests were primarily feasibility tests and included clients from only a few months' intakes. The pilot test data themselves were thus of limited use for agency decisionmaking purposes. Also, without outcome data from more than one time period, some major uses of outcome data that depend on trends and changes over time could not be attempted.

As part of the pilot tests, however, we developed a number of illustrative analyses and data summaries using the pilot test data. These summaries served as the basis for discussions with pilot test agency managers and supervisors regarding applications of outcome data. These discussions supported our expectation that outcome data are urgently needed and will be used. Even a small amount of test data stimulated many questions about service priorities and training. Agency managers were excited about the prospect of having data to support or refute policies that had been made in the absence of systematic outcome data. Several of these summaries and the results of some of the discussions are presented in this chapter to illustrate ways in which client outcome information can be analyzed and used. At the end of the chapter we also point out some important limitations on the interpretation and use of outcome data.

## Uses for Client Outcome Information

The following eight uses for client outcome information are discussed:

- Budget preparation and justification and resource allocation

- Program evaluation and cost-effectiveness studies

- Assessment of patterns and trends in client needs

- Assessment of individual clients

- Performance targets for contractors and employees

- Quality assurance and staffing standards

- Obtaining client input

- Providing feedback to staff on overall outcomes

1. <u>Budget Preparation and Justification and Resource Allocation</u>. Social services agencies currently must decide whether to expand programs, cut back programs, or fund new programs without the benefit, for the most part, of even crude information on how clients fare after services. They must face governors, mayors, city and county managers, legislatures, and the public without any outcome information to support claims for the efficacy of services and requests for funds. The data collected using these procedures can provide systematic information both on the distribution of client needs (from the pre-service interviews) and on outcomes and areas where client problems remain unsolved despite current services.

2. <u>Program Evaluations and Cost-Effectiveness Studies</u>. Outcome data can constitute one component of program evaluation and cost-effectiveness studies, along with data on service activity, program characteristics, costs, and other factors influencing outcomes. For some studies, data from an ongoing outcome monitoring effort can be used directly. For example, a study of counseling services might utilize past years' outcome data for clients that had received these services.

In some studies that require special information on client outcomes, these procedures, if already institutionalized, could be used to obtain the information more quickly than would otherwise be possible. If an agency were collecting regular outcome information on all or a large proportion of its clients, experiments using randomly selected experimental and control groups would be more feasible, since procedures for obtaining outcome data on both groups would already be in place.

Even if they are not already in place, these procedures can be initiated for special studies. For example, North Carolina has used the procedures and modified portions of the questionnaire for a study of chore and homemaker services to disabled and elderly clients.

Outcome data can be used to select programs for in-depth evaluation. The evaluation of programs with particularly good or poor outcomes can provide insights into what service delivery methods or organizational structures work well and should be expanded and what methods work poorly and should be discarded or modified. When outcomes are collected over several years, "norms" can be developed for outcomes, and programs whose outcomes deviate from these norms can be targeted for examination. Also, comparison of outcomes from year to year can provide clues to the effects of major changes in service programs or in the external environment in which services are delivered.

3. <u>Assessment of Patterns and Trends in Client Needs</u>. Aggregated data from the pre-service interviews will provide systematic information on the characteristics and problems of incoming clients. Agency officials can use this information to track patterns and changes over time in incoming clients and their service needs. This information can be used to provide guidance on what types and quantities of services and staff will be required to meet client needs. It can also be used to pinpoint geographical areas or client groups where needs are more urgent and where more services should be concentrated.

4. <u>Assessment of Individual Clients</u>. Information from pre-service interviews can supplement information obtained in regular casework intake interviews. Casework intake interviews often focus on the main presenting

problem, with time and priority constraints preventing more comprehensive assessments. While the pre-service monitoring interview is not intended to be an in-depth interview, it touches on a broad range of client functioning and can alert caseworkers to problems and basic functioning outside of the immediate presenting problem.

5. <u>Performance Targets for Contractors and Employees</u>. Once sufficient experience has been gained with outcome information, it can be used to provide a basis for performance targets for program managers, such as where management-by-objectives (MBO) programs are used, or for "performance contracts" for providers of contracted services. If used constructively, outcome-based performance targets can serve as incentives, with or without monetary rewards, for managers and contractors to seek program improvements.

6. <u>Quality Assurance and Staffing Standards</u>. An increasing number of standards for staffing, training, and service activity are being instituted or advocated in social services. Many standards are controversial and costly. Outcome data can provide a basis for choosing meaningful standards. It makes little sense to set "quality of care" standards without reference to outcomes. Until agencies can determine what types of education, training, and experience make a difference in outcomes, and what staff-to-client ratios produce acceptable outcomes, there is little basis for setting staffing policy.

7. <u>Obtaining Client Input</u>. The procedures solicit clients' perceptions of how well needs were met and the quality of services, both overall and on specific factors such as timeliness and courtesy and the helpfulness of specific services. (These opinions are in addition to the data on client problems before and after services that are used to more "objectively" measure outcomes.) Clients thus are given a formal opportunity to tell the agency their perceptions about services.

8. <u>Feedback to Staff on Overall Outcomes</u>. Aggregate data can be provided to all staff, to let them see how clients fare after agency services and how satisfied clients feel. The feedback could be made part of "how are we doing" meetings at which staff members discuss services and how they might be improved.

## Illustrative Outcome Data Summaries

The pilot tests included preparation of a number of illustrative summary displays of the pilot test data and discussions of these data. Some of the displays shown here include composite data from the pilot tests (we have not identified which data belong to which agency in order to protect the agencies' confidentiality). The data are based on small samples in two agencies for short periods of time and are not presented as being representative of outcomes in these agencies. The data are shown for illustrative purposes only. The summary displays shown in this chapter include several that we recommend as basic displays to state and local agencies implementing outcome measurement procedures.

The data summaries fall into three major categories:

- <u>Client outcomes after receiving services</u>. How much did clients' problems change from before to after services? What are the outcomes for different types of clients, different years, similar programs in different organizational units or different facilities, and different treatment approaches?

- Clients' perceptions of the helpfulness and quality of services. How satisfied were the clients with the services and the agency? To what extent did they think services helped them?

- Description of clients and their problems. Who were the clients? What problems did they present? What services did they receive?

Summaries for each of these three categories are discussed and illustrated in the following sections:

1. Client Outcomes After Receiving Services

Summary Display #1 - Outcomes by Major Service Divisions (Exhibit 14)

This is a basic summary that presents outcome data for each of an agency's major service divisions. It shows the percentages of clients whose problems improved, were unchanged, and worsened in each problem area and in all problem areas combined. A parallel display could show outcomes for similar service divisions in different agencies (for example, for family services in several counties), or for several supervisory units within a division, or for different contractors for a specific service.

This summary provides a "scorecard" on outcomes. These data can point out areas where outcomes seem particularly high or low compared to average outcomes. Special attention could then be given to determining how outcomes in "low" areas can be improved, and to identifying what might be causing "high" outcomes. For example, the data in Exhibit 14 indicate low percentages of improvement for client problems with basic activities of living, child-problem behavior, and alcohol and drug abuse. It would be worthwhile to explore whether these problems showed low percentages improved in all units or all agencies, perhaps indicating that these problems were generally intractable and high levels of improvement should not be expected, or whether some units or agencies showed better results than others, indicating that they possess successful service methods that should be identified and applied elsewhere.

Summary Display #2 - Outcomes by Severity of Pre-Service Problems (Exhibit 15)

While Display #1 can provide gross indicators of particularly high and low outcomes that require attention, it can be misleading unless the agency considers differences in the severity of initial problems. Otherwise, a higher percentage of improvement for one unit compared to another could reflect inherent differences in the caseloads rather than differences in service effectiveness. Therefore, outcomes should also be displayed, as they are in Exhibit 15, by severity of client problem before services. This illustrative display shows data on overall client condition for different service divisions; similar displays could show the data for individual problem areas, and for different facilities, contractors, or supervisory units. When different providers use different approaches, a display such as this can help to more fairly assess which approaches appear to produce better outcomes.

## EXHIBIT 14

## SUMMARY DISPLAY #1.  OUTCOMES BY MAJOR SERVICE DIVISIONS

| Service Division[a] | Change | Physical Health % | Activities of Daily Living % | Mental Distress % | Family Strength % | Alcohol or Drug Abuse % | Child Problem Behavior % | Physical Abuse % | Poverty % | Dependence on Welfare % | Change Across All Problem Areas % |
|---|---|---|---|---|---|---|---|---|---|---|---|
| Family Services | Improved | 32 | 29 | 38 | 40 | 44 | 28 | 100 | 48 | 35 | 43 |
| | Unchanged | 34 | 0 | 28 | 28 | 0 | 31 | 0 | 35 | 49 | 15 |
| | Worsened | 34 | 71 | 34 | 32 | 56 | 41 | 0 | 17 | 16 | 43 |
| n= | | | | | | | | (Only 1 client had problem) | | | |
| Adult Services | Improved | 47 | 32 | 52 | 37 | 0 | 50 | 0 | 50 | 31 | 58 |
| | Unchanged | 39 | 23 | 37 | 26 | 0 | 50 | 0 | 36 | 46 | 11 |
| | Worsened | 14 | 45 | 11 | 37 | 100 | 0 | 100 | 14 | 23 | 31 |
| n= | | | | | | (Only 3 clients had problem) | (Only 2 clients had problem) | (Only 1 client had problem) | | | |
| Both Divisions | Improved | 39 | 31 | 44 | 39 | 33 | 29 | 50 | 49 | 33 | 51 |
| | Unchanged | 37 | 17 | 32 | 27 | 0 | 32 | 0 | 37 | 48 | 13 |
| | Worsened | 24 | 52 | 24 | 34 | 67 | 39 | 50 | 14 | 19 | 36 |
| n= | | | | | | (Only 2 clients had problem) | | (Only 2 clients had problem) | | | |

Of clients who had problems in each area, either pre-service or at followup, what percentage improved, stayed the same, and worsened?

a.  The numbers of clients are not shown in this illustrative display, to preserve the confidentiality of the pilot test agencies.  In an actual display, numbers should be shown, and the number of "no problem" cases and cases in which the outcomes are unknown (missing data) or not applicable should be shown also for each box in the table to provide readers with the base on which the percentages are calculated.

EXHIBIT 15

SUMMARY DISPLAY #2.  OUTCOMES BY SEVERITY OF PRE-SERVICE PROBLEMS

| Overall Pre-Service Problem Severity | Change from Pre-Service to Follow-up | Family Services[a] % | Adult Services[a] % | Total, Both Divisions[a] % |
|---|---|---|---|---|
| Minor Problems | Improved | 25 | 50 | 33 |
| | Unchanged | 50 | 50 | 50 |
| | Worsened | 25 | 0 | 17 |
| | | n= | n= | n= |
| Moderate Problems | Improved | 30 | 54 | 42 |
| | Unchanged | 17 | 14 | 16 |
| | Worsened | 53 | 32 | 42 |
| | | n= | n= | n= |
| Major Problems | Improved | 69 | 61 | 65 |
| | Unchanged | 0 | 8 | 4 |
| | Worsened | 31 | 31 | 31 |
| | | n= | n= | n= |
| Total, all pre-service severities | Improved | 43 | 56 | 50 |
| | Unchanged | 14 | 14 | 14 |
| | Worsened | 43 | 30 | 36 |
| | | n= | n= | n= |

a.  The number of clients are not shown in this illustrative display to preserve the confidentiality of the pilot test agencies.  In an actual display, numbers should be shown.

Summary Display #3 - Outcomes by Client Demographic Characteristics (Exhibit 16)

This exhibit shows improvement rates in two problem areas--family strength and mental distress--for different sex, race, and age groups. Similar displays could be made for any other client characteristics for which data are collected. Such information can help agencies to assess whether particular programs or treatment approaches work better with some groups than others. The information can be used to assess whether some client groups have particularly poor outcomes and might warrant special attention.

Information such as this can also be used, along with information on severity of problems (such as Display #2), to explore the question of client "difficulty." Some clients and some problems are easier to help than others. Severity of problems at intake is one factor, but there are other factors that influence the effectiveness of services and these should be considered when measuring outcomes. For example, in the mental health field there is some evidence that outcomes of counseling may be correlated with educational levels. Some other client characteristics such as age may also contribute to "difficulty." After outcome data have been collected over a substantial length of time, it should be possible to develop norms for expected outcomes that are related to specific client characteristics and problem severity. These norms would provide a basis for identifying especially good or poor outcome rates.

Summary Display #4 - Outcome Trends over Time (Exhibit 17)

After data have been collected for more than one period of time, time trends can be identified. If major program changes have been introduced in one period, the outcome data for the next period will indicate whether outcomes have improved following these changes (but, as noted elsewhere, this evidence would not be sufficient to determine definitely whether the program changes actually caused the observed changes in outcomes).

The pilot tests described in this report obtained outcome data for only one period of time and, thus, no illustrative time trend data are available from those tests. Exhibit 17, however, shows a format that might be used to summarize time trend data.

Summary Display #5 - Outcomes by Services Received (Exhibit 18)

How are outcomes related to the type and amount of service? Although outcome data by themselves do not show to what extent services cause the observed outcomes, this summary display can help explore possible connections. Since the type and amount of service received is likely to be related to the nature and severity of the client's problem at intake, displays that summarize outcomes by services received should probably at the same time show outcomes by pre-service condition or presenting problems. Exhibit 18 illustrates a format for displaying outcomes relative to different amounts of service and different pre-service problem severities. Similar tables could show outcomes for different types of service, for different presenting problems, and for a combination of different presenting problems and severities.

EXHIBIT 16

SUMMARY DISPLAY #3.  OUTCOMES BY CLIENT DEMOGRAPHIC CHARACTERISTICS

Of clients who had problems, either pre-service or at follow up, what percentage improved, stayed the same, or worsened?[a]

| Characteristic | | Family Strength | | | Mental Distress | | | All Problem Areas Combined | | |
|---|---|---|---|---|---|---|---|---|---|---|
| | | Improved % | Unchanged % | Worsened % | Improved % | Unchanged % | Worsened % | Improved % | Unchanged % | Worsened % |
| Sex | Male n= | 13 | 37 | 50 | 17 | 50 | 33 | 41 | 6 | 53 |
| | Female n= | 34 | 28 | 38 | 48 | 30 | 22 | 53 | 13 | 34 |
| Race | White n= | 46 | 27 | 27 | 55 | 27 | 18 | 41 | 16 | 43 |
| | Black and Other n= | 23 | 31 | 46 | 38 | 36 | 26 | 56 | 10 | 34 |
| Age | 0-17 n= | 17 | 33 | 50 | 0 | 33 | 67 | 50 | 29 | 21 |
| | 18-34 n= | 30 | 30 | 40 | 50 | 31 | 19 | 43 | 7 | 50 |
| | 35-64 n= | 33 | 33 | 33 | 33 | 38 | 29 | 52 | 8 | 40 |
| | 65+ n= | 75 | 0 | 25 | 67 | 22 | 11 | 72 | 21 | 7 |
| Total, all clients | | 32 | 29 | 39 | 45 | 32 | 23 | 51 | 12 | 37 |

a.  Numbers of clients are not shown in this illustrative display to protect the confidentiality of the pilot test agencies.  Numbers of clients, and numbers of clients with "no problem," "unknown," or "not applicable," in each box in the table would be shown in an actual display.

## EXHIBIT 17

### SUMMARY DISPLAY #4.  OUTCOME TRENDS OVER TIME

| Pre-Service Problem Severity | Change from Pre-Service to Follow-up | 1978 % | 1979 % | 1980 % |
|---|---|---|---|---|
| Minor Problems | Improved Unchanged Worsened | | | |
| Moderate Problems | Improved Unchanged Worsened | | | |
| Major Problems | Improved Unchanged Worsened | | | |
| Total, all pre-service severities | Improved Unchanged Worsened | | | |

EXHIBIT 18

SUMMARY DISPLAY #5.  OUTCOMES BY SERVICES RECEIVED

| Severity of Problems Pre-Service | Percentage of Family Services Clients Whose Problems Improved[a] | | | |
|---|---|---|---|---|
| | Service Level 1 | Service Level 2 | Service Level 3 | Service Level 4 |
| Minor Problems | | | | |
| Moderate Problems | | | | |
| Major Problems | | | | |
| Total, all severities | | | | |

    a.  "Service Levels" could be defined by intensity, length, or amount of service--for example, 1 interview, 2-5 interviews, 6-20 interviews, more than 20 interviews between pre-service and follow up.

Such tables can give clues as to what types and amounts of service seem to lead to the best outcomes, given particular types and levels of problems. They should also provide useful guidance to agency officials for staffing allocations.

Difficulties in analyzing and interpreting outcomes by services will arise since clients frequently receive several services simultaneously or in succession between pre-service and follow-up interviews. Clients may also receive services from other sources in the community. In all these cases, the outcomes related to each individual service will be difficult, if not impossible, to separate out--regardless of the outcome assessment procedures used. Given a sufficiently large sample size, statistical procedures such as analysis of covariance can provide clues about the differential effects of individual services or groups of services. However, some services are naturally linked together--for example, most clients who receive homemaker services may also receive health-related services--so that separating out individual service effects would be impossible.

Where multiple services are present, any data-collection procedure short of use of "controlled experimental designs" will inevitably find great difficulty in isolating the effects of any one service.

If an agency has cost accounting procedures that provide treatment costs for individual clients, these can be aggregated for various groups of clients such as those in different programs and different problem levels. This would permit calculation of cost-effectiveness ratios for each group, that is, calculation of the "costs per improved client" for each group of clients. Comparisons of such unit costs, both among programs, among types of clients, and over time, would provide agency officials with considerable guidance for decisions on resource allocation. A substantial limitation that currently exists in social service agencies, however, is the lack of cost-accounting procedures that provide accurate estimates of staff time and dollars spent on individual clients.

### Summary Display #6 - Changes in Average Client Condition (Exhibit 19)

In addition to displaying outcomes in terms of proportion of clients improved, average severity of client problems at follow up can be compared to average severity at intake. A graphic format for displaying before and after averages is shown in Exhibit 19.

This type of graphic display is one possible format for presenting outcome data to caseworkers. Feedback to caseworkers is an important use of outcome data. One of the frustrations of social casework is not knowing about the outcomes of the work, particularly how well client gains are sustained after termination. Follow-up data on individual clients, particularly satisfaction data, probably should not be provided to caseworkers because of confidentiality requirements. Caseworkers, however, can be provided with data aggregated at the supervisory unit level or higher, including the summaries shown in this chapter. Exhibit 19 illustrates (with fictitious data) a graphic display of outcomes that might be an effective means of letting caseworkers see client outcomes.

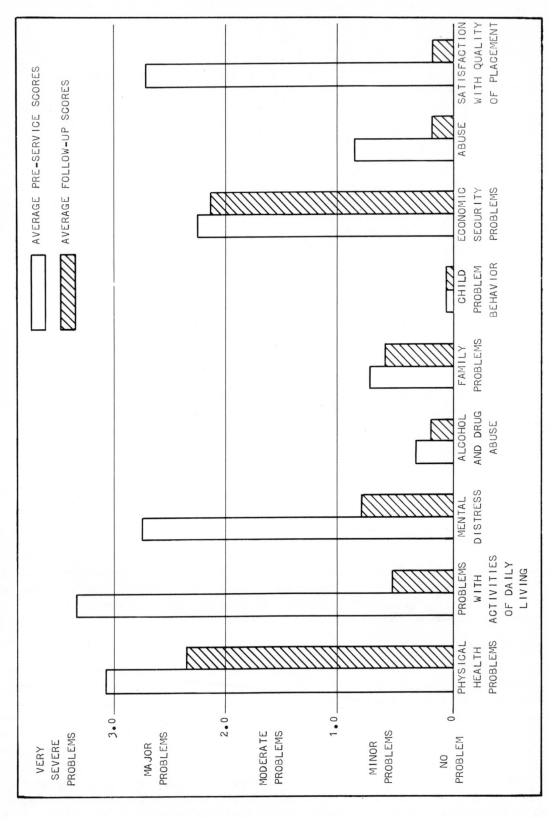

EXHIBIT 19

SUMMARY DISPLAY #6. CHANGES IN AVERAGE CLIENT CONDITION

NOTE: Fictitious data for adult services.

Feedback on this and the other exhibits might be given in "how are we doing" reviews to facilitate communication between staff and management and stimulate discussion of ways to improve services.

2. Clients' Perceptions of the Helpfulness and Quality of Services

Summary Display #7 - Client Satisfaction with Services (Exhibit 20)

The client interviews ask for clients' perceptions of how their problems changed in severity since starting service, whether they feel services helped alleviate their problems, and how satisfied they were with specific aspects of the quality of services such as accessibility and staff courteousness. Findings can be presented in a format like that shown in Exhibit 20. This exhibit summarizes client responses to selected questions for each service division. Similar displays can be presented to show clients' satisfaction with specific services.

When clients indicate dissatisfaction with some aspect of services, they are asked to describe the specific reason for the dissatisfaction. These responses can also be tabulated, to help the agency identify ways to improve service delivery.

These "satisfaction" data provide the clients' perceptions of outcomes and of the quality of services, and thus provide another perspective from which to view the more "objective" outcome results.

3. Description of Clients and Their Problems

Summary Display #8 - Pre-service Problems and Services Received, by Principal "Presenting Problem" (Exhibit 21)

These data come from the pre-service interviews and from agency records on services provided to clients. This particular illustration shows data for the clients of a family services unit.

Such information can help an agency assess the incidence of various problems among incoming clients so it can better match its services to its clients' problems. For example, Exhibit 21 indicates that help with emergency financial problems was the most common request. It also shows that clients commonly reported serious problems in one or more areas besides the primary one for which they were requesting services. Problems with children, with health, with family relationships, and with mental and emotional well being were frequently reported. In one of the pilot agencies, which was faced with possible severe cuts in funding for services that were not legally mandated, the findings shown in a display similar to this one indicated that most clients appeared to be seeking primarily nonmandated services that might not be available in the near future. Alterations in service funding to more closely fit the pattern of client demands should be considered. The findings also stimulated discussion of the need for a more efficient and effective approach to emergency financial needs. One of the pilot agencies did not have funds from the state for financial emergencies such as threatened evictions or utility shutoffs. The agency caseworkers had to spend a lot of time seeking money for clients from churches and other community sources. Perhaps it would be more cost effective to provide public money for client emergency needs, rather than paying for the caseworker time required to seek funds elsewhere.

EXHIBIT 20

## SUMMARY DISPLAY #7.  CLIENT SATISFACTION WITH SERVICES

| Service Division [a] | In general, considering all your contacts with the Social Service Bureau and all services you received since we first interviewed you, how satisfied do you feel with the Bureau? | % | Have you had any problems with the delay time between arriving for services and actually getting services? | % | Have you had any problems getting in touch with social workers when you needed to talk with them or see them? | % | Have you had any problems with the way the people at the Social Services Bureau treated you--for example, have they been polite and have they paid attention to you? | % | Overall, do you feel that the services you received from the Social Services Bureau had any effect - good or bad - on your problems? | % |
|---|---|---|---|---|---|---|---|---|---|---|
| Family | Very satisfied | 50 | | | | | | | | |
| | Somewhat satisfied | 32 | | | | | | | | |
| n= | Neutral | 8 | No problem | 85 | No problem | 80 | No problem | 90 | Good effect | 48 |
| | Somewhat dissatisfied | 10 | Minor problem | 5 | Minor problem | 7 | Minor problem | 5 | No effect | 48 |
| | Very dissatisfied | 0 | Moderate problem | 0 | Moderate problem | 3 | Moderate problem | 0 | Bad effect | 2 |
| | | | Major problem | 10 | Major problem | 10 | Major problem | 5 | | |
| Adult | Very satisfied | 54 | | | | | | | | |
| | Somewhat satisfied | 16 | | | | | | | | |
| n= | Neutral | 11 | No problem | 70 | No problem | 89 | No problem | 94 | Good effect | 56 |
| | Somewhat dissatisfied | 14 | Minor problem | 5 | Minor problem | 11 | Minor problem | 3 | No effect | 38 |
| | Very dissatisfied | 5 | Moderate problem | 3 | Moderate problem | 0 | Moderate problem | 0 | Bad effect | 3 |
| | | | Major problem (1 unknown) | 19 | Major problem | 0 | Major problem | 3 | Mixed - good and bad | 3 |
| Total | Very satisfied | 51 | | | | | | | | |
| | Somewhat satisfied | 25 | | | | | | | | |
| n= | Neutral | 9 | No problem | 80 | No problem | 85 | No problem | 92 | Good effect | 53 |
| | Somewhat dissatisfied | 12 | Minor problem | 5 | Minor problem | 9 | Minor problem | 4 | No effect | 43 |
| | Very dissatisfied | 3 | Moderate problem | 1 | Moderate problem | 1 | Moderate problem | 0 | Bad effect | 3 |
| | | | Major problem | 14 | Major problem | 5 | Major problem | 4 | Mixed - good and bad | 1 |

a.  Numbers of clients are not included in this illustrative display, to protect the pilot test agencies' confidentiality.  In an actual display, numbers would be shown.

## EXHIBIT 21

### SUMMARY DISPLAY #8. PRE-SERVICE PROBLEMS AND SERVICES RECEIVED, BY PRINCIPAL "PRESENTING PROBLEM"

| Primary "Presenting Problem" Named by Client | Problem Level Pre-Service | Percentage of Family Services Clients Reporting Problems in Each Problem Area | | | | | | | | Services Received (and No. of Clients Receiving Each Service)[a] |
|---|---|---|---|---|---|---|---|---|---|---|
| | | Physical Health % | Activities of Daily Living % | Mental Distress % | Family Strength % | Alcohol or Drug Abuse % | Child Problem Behavior % | Physical Abuse % | Poverty or Dependence on Welfare % | |
| Financial emergency | Major or very severe | 10 | 5 | 30 | 5 | 5 | 10 | | 55 | Emergency (30), case management (10), health counseling (9), housing (8), court (7), day care (6), employment (5), education (4), family planning (3), protective (2), nutrition (1), WIN (2) |
| | Moderate | 35 | 5 | 25 | 25 | 0 | 20 | 0 | 45 | |
| | Minor | 40 | 0 | 15 | 15 | 15 | 35 | 0 | 0 | |
| 45 clients[a] | No problem | 15 | 90 | 30 | 55 | 80 | 35 | 95 | 0 | |
| Health problems | Major or very severe | 20 | 0 | 40 | 20 | 0 | 20 | 0 | 40 | Case management (10), health (15), counseling (5), housing (4), court (2), day care (2), socialization (2), transportation(6) |
| | Moderate | 20 | 20 | 0 | 20 | 0 | 40 | 0 | 40 | |
| | Minor | 60 | 0 | 40 | 0 | 0 | 20 | 0 | 20 | |
| 20 clients[a] | No problem | 0 | 80 | 20 | 60 | 100 | 20 | 100 | 0 | |
| . . . | | | | | | | | | | |
| Total, all presenting problems | Major or very severe | 8 | 3 | 25 | 10 | 3 | 10 | 3 | 53 | |
| | Moderate | 30 | 5 | 18 | 20 | 3 | 28 | 0 | 44 | |
| | Minor | 45 | 0 | 25 | 13 | 10 | 28 | 0 | 3 | |
| ___ clients | No problem | 17 | 92 | 32 | 58 | 84 | 34 | 97 | 0 | |

a. The number of clients shown in this illustrative display are fictitious, to protect the pilot test agencies' confidentiality.

The data in the exhibit show that many clients received more and different services than those needed for the primary presenting problem. Focusing only on the presenting problem and on a single service would probably result in missing important outcomes.

Summary Display #9 - Psychosocial Summary (Exhibit 22)

This exhibit illustrates a potential byproduct of monitoring. Although the primary purpose of monitoring is to provide information for program planning and other management decisionmaking, pre-service data on individual clients can also be provided to caseworkers to help them in determining client needs.[1] When a client presents specific urgent problems there may not be time in the intake interview to explore functioning in other areas of the client's life. In some cases there is never an opportunity for such exploration, due to the pressures on caseworkers' time. The information obtained from the pre-service interviews might be provided to workers in a format such as the "psychosocial summary" shown in the exhibit, or in a simpler list form. Agencies with computers or word-processing equipment could generate such summaries at least partly automatically from the intake questionnaires.

## Need for and Source of "Norms" for Comparing Current Performances

Outcome information will be more informative when "norms," or standards, are available that indicate what outcomes can be expected. Since outcome data are currently rare, there are generally no existing norms against which observed outcomes can be compared. When outcome data are collected for several years, it will be possible to develop norms for "expected" outcomes.

Meanwhile, agencies that want to set outcome "performance targets" (such as in management-by-objective programs) could base them on the previous year's outcomes and on outcomes for other programs or facilities that are similar in function and, perhaps, have relatively high performance. Such targets should reflect relevant client characteristics including severity and difficulty of client problems that are likely to differ from program to program and from year to year.

Another source of "norms" is data on functioning levels of a sample of the general population. This approach has sometimes been used to help assess

---

1. We advise against providing caseworkers with individual client follow-up information. Informed consent rules require that clients be told if their caseworkers are going to see the data; this could have a major influence on clients' responses, particularly on the satisfaction questions. Client concern about caseworkers seeing the responses seems less of a problem for the pre-service interviews which focus on identifying client functioning levels. However, there is a possibility that responses could be affected. Clients who are applying for financial aid, or whose children are being considered for removal from the home, might want to withhold some information from caseworkers. Since pre-service interviewing data on individual clients were not provided to caseworkers, in our pilot tests, we have no evidence regarding possible effects on client responses.

EXHIBIT 22

SUMMARY DISPLAY #9. PSYCHOSOCIAL SUMMARY

---

Client: Mrs. X
Date of Interview: April 1, 1980

Presenting Problem: The client is a 47-year-old white woman who came to the agency for "medical assistance."

Background: Client finished the 9th grade in school. She is separated from her husband and lives with her adult daughter.

In the past month:

Physical Health: Client's health is "poor" and gives her major functioning problems. She was too sick to carry on her usual activities more than 14 days of the past month. She has major problems getting medical care; she has no medical insurance and needs help to pay hospital bills.

Mental Distress: She is often fearful, angry, confused, and tense, and often has trouble sleeping due to worries. She almost always feels depressed and very tired. Once or twice she has had headaches and poor appetite. She never has an upset stomach. She has felt suicidal once or twice, and often feels lonely.

Alcohol and Drug Abuse: Client reports no drinking problem. She had not had a drink in the past month. She reported no drug use and no drug problem.

Family Strength: Client reports major problems with family and close friends who do not live with her, with arguments between herself and the daughter who lives with her, and with feeling close to her daughter. There are minor problems with her daughter's drinking.

Activities of Daily Living: She reports no difficulty with personal care, but has trouble doing her housework, doing shopping if it involves more than one or two things, and doing laundry. She has no difficulty cooking or traveling beyond walking distance (she takes the bus) or taking medicine. Her daughter and a neighbor help with housework, shopping, and laundry, by carrying things.

Economic Self-Support: Client has major problems with paying bills and with the condition of her housing. She did not work at all during the past 3 months, and is unemployed and looking for work currently. She has been unable to find work because no jobs were available. Her daughter brings home $300 a month, and this, plus a $20 birthday gift to the client, was the household's total income last month. They receive no welfare or food stamps.

Other Comments by Client: Client's husband has health problems (stroke). She has had problems with relationships with her children and worries about her daughter's safety.

---

NOTE:   Information obtained from pre-service evaluation questionnaire.
        Underlined items are client responses.

mental distress levels.  Mental distress norms are already available for the mental health questions shown in Appendix 1 and are discussed further in Appendix 2.

### Limitations to the Interpretation and the Use of Outcome Data

Two important concerns regarding the interpretation and use of client outcome data are discussed in this section:  (1) Outcome data by themselves cannot adequately assess the extent to which agency services, rather than other factors, bring about the observed outcomes.  (2) The quality of the data-collection procedures must be carefully maintained to avoid deterioration in the validity of the data.

Lack of cause-effect information.  The outcome monitoring procedures presented in this report provide data on clients' problems before services, clients' problems after services, changes in problems from before services to after services, and the type and amount of services provided to each client. Correlations between services and outcomes can be made.  However, the services provided cannot be assumed to bear a cause-and-effect relationship to the changes because of the variety of other factors that can affect outcomes. Outside factors, and time itself, may in some instances lead to alleviation of client problems.[1]

Outcome data do not necessarily show the "results" of services because differences in client outcomes over time may result from circumstances such as changes in economic conditions and employment opportunities, disasters, epidemics, and bad winters.  Staff should keep track of such factors and consider them when interpreting outcomes.

More in-depth evaluation studies such as controlled experiments are needed to provide definitive information on the cause-and-effect relationships between services and outcomes.  Outcome procedures such as those presented here can provide the outcome data in such special studies.  The costs and difficulties involved in these in-depth studies, however, mean that agencies will seldom be able to undertake them, and then only on a small scale with specific services.  For the most part, public officials who wish to evaluate programs will have to rely on less rigorous information such as that provided by outcome monitoring.[2]

---

1.  In essence, the designs built into our outcome monitoring procedures include a "pretest-posttest" design, "natural" comparison groups of clients receiving different services, and a time-series design (which requires the periodic measurement of outcomes over time, a feature of the proposed approach).  The approach also includes a provision for statistical "control" of selected client characteristics, including the condition of the client at intake.

2.  As noted earlier, if an agency were collecting regular outcome information on all or a large proportion of clients, controlled experiments would become considerably more feasible, since procedures for obtaining substantial "before" and "after" information on "experimental" and "control" groups of

(continued)

When outcomes are being compared (for state-level analysis) for different agencies at different locations, interpretations should allow for local factors not under the control of social services, such as poor public transportation, housing shortages, and high unemployment.

Outcomes will also be influenced by the type and severity of client problems at intake. As discussed, this factor should be explicitly considered when comparing outcomes between one unit and another, or over time.

Possible sources of error in the procedures and need for periodic "audits" of the data-collection procedures. There are a number of possible sources for errors and biases in the outcome information. Problems in the procedures for identifying new clients, for obtaining client consent, and for locating clients for pre-service and follow-up interviews, as well as poor interviewing practices, can distort outcome data and lead to faulty interpretations. Agencies should conduct periodic "audits" of the quality of the data-collection procedures and the accuracy of the data. If, for example, refusals and failures to locate clients exceed, say, 50 percent, the procedures should be reexamined to see if corrections can be made. Technical assistance may be helpful in establishing good quality procedures and in periodically reviewing their adequacy.

## Final Comment

The procedures discussed in this report are not perfect. They will be improved as more experience is gained with them and as the general "state of the art" of social services outcome measurement improves.

Currently, most state and local social service agencies entirely lack systematic, regularly collected, objective information on client outcomes. Even partially tested procedures such as those discussed here will provide data that will be better than what now exists. If outcome data are regularly collected, with adequate attention to the data quality control, and if agency officials spend the time and effort necessary to use the data, then outcome monitoring will provide vital information on service performance. This information can greatly help social service officials make more effective use of agency funds.

---

clients would already be in place. Outcome monitoring could contribute to the evaluation of experiments involving, for example, changes in caseload sizes, changes in the proportions of professionally trained and nonprofessionally trained caseworkers, or changes in methods such as from individual to group treatment.

# APPENDIX 1.

## ILLUSTRATIVE CLIENT

## OUTCOME QUESTIONNAIRE

Note:  See Appendices 2-4 for discussion
of the questionnaire's content
and tests of its validity.

# Notes on the Questionnaire

## Coding

The answer categories for most questions are pre-coded for direct key-punching from the questionnaire. The code numbers "8" and "9" are reserved for "missing" and "don't know" responses, respectively. (The coordinator would code "8," for example, when an interviewer had mistakenly skipped a question.) "0" means "inapplicable" in most cases. Some questions with open-ended or complex responses are not pre-coded; the coordinator must code these, using coding guides, after the interviews are completed.

We have not put in the column numbers, but have indicated how many columns are reserved for each response. For example, ( , ) indicates that two columns are required and ( , , ) means that three columns are required.

## Face Sheet

In the pilot tests, each interviewer should be provided with a "face sheet" attached to the front of the questionnaire for each client. The face sheet should give the information required for contacting clients, tell whether the clients are in substitute care, and whether the respondent lives in the same household as the client (information required for skip instructions within the questionnaire). In addition, interviewers should be asked to record the effort made to reach the client, the time required for the interview, and any special comments about the interview.

## From Records

In addition to information collected in the client interview, some items are needed from agency and client records, such as

### Information on Services for Analysis (to cross-tabulate with outcomes)

--List of all services given to client between intake and present time
--Eligibility category
--Was client receiving financial assistance, medicaid, or food stamps at intake for services? At present time?
--Date first service delivered
--Date of last caseworker contact and/or service delivery

--Number of telephone and in-person contacts (if this is available in
  records)
--Whether case is open or closed at time of follow up
--Date case closed (if closed) (most recent closing)
--Reason case closed (most recent closing)
--Title XX goal history and status at termination (most recent termination)


Information on Outcomes (to compare with client responses on questionnaire)

--Was there a report of abuse within six months before intake?  Between
  intake and present time?  Was it confirmed?  Who abused whom (relationships, not names)?
--Did the client have a drinking or drug problem at intake?  At the
  present time?
--Was client in substitute care at intake?  What type of substitute care?
  Is client in substitute care at this time?  What type?  How many changes
  in living arrangements (different placements, returns to own home, etc.)
  have there been between intake and present time?


## Scoring

The following scoring procedure was used to summarize the pilot test questionnaire data.

Weights were assigned to answer choices following a consistent pattern:
1=minor problem, 3=moderate problem, 6=major problem, and 15=especially severe
or important problem.  Most questions' answer weight ranged only up to 6, with
15 being reserved for the following very severe or important problems:  abuse
by family members with police intervention or need for medical care; almost
always contemplating suicide; having five or more drinks nearly every day;
responding with three or four "yes" replies on the CAGE scale (an indicator of
alcoholism); being arrested in connection with drinking; admitted drinking problem; taking hard drugs nearly every day; being arrested in connection with drugs;
admitted drug problem; children committing vandalism or stealing; being bed-
bound; being unable to travel without an ambulance; having an income below
50 percent of the poverty line.  Answers of "no problem," "no," and "never"
were counted as "0," as were nonapplicable questions.

The number score for each module was the sum of the weights.  The letter
score for each module was derived directly from the sum, based on an algorithm
which took into account both number and severity of problems.  As a general
rule*

     0 = A = no problem       = no problems

     1-2 = B = minor problem   = one or two minor problems

---

*Mental Distress used a different scale.

3-8 = C = moderate problem = three to eight minor problems or one to two moderate problems or one major problem (or various combinations of one or two moderate or one major and some minors)

9-14 = D = major problem = nine to fourteen minor problems or three or four moderate problems or two major problems (or combinations of one or two major problems, or several lesser problems)

15+ = E = very severe problem = five moderate problems or more than two major problems or one very severe problem (or combinations of problems adding up to more than 15 points)

Detailed scoring procedures are available for each module (but are not included with this illustrative questionnaire).

Change scores were derived by subtracting the follow-up score from the pre-service score. Thus a client who went from a number score of 6 at intake to a number score of 15 at follow up and from a letter score of C at intake to a letter score of E at follow up had a number change of -9 and a letter change of -2. (Further work with the data will be required to decide whether it is more valid to base change on number change or letter change.)

| BACKGROUND INFORMATION | ( , , )_ _ _ Client I.D. |
|---|---|
| | ( ) 1 Intake |
| | 2 Follow-up |
| | ( ) ① Questionnaire Version |
| | ( , )01 Module Number |

---

1. (Relationship of Respondent to Client)                    ( , ) 01 Self

---

Thank you for agreeing to have this interview.  First there
are a few background questions.

2.  What is your age?                                        ( , )_ _ Exact Age in Years

---

CIRCLE RESPONDENT'S SEX.
ASK ONLY IF NOT OBVIOUS.

3.  What is your sex?                                        ( ) 1 Male
                                                                 2 Female

---

IF CLIENT LIVES IN GROUP RESIDENCE
OR INSTITUTION, SKIP TO Q. 5.

4.  Counting yourself, how many people live in your household    ( , )_ _ Number of persons
    at this time?                                                         in household (00
                                                                          if group residence
                                                                          or institution)

   a.  How many of the people in your household are adults
       age 18 or older?                                         ( , )_ _ Number of adults

   b.  How many of the people in your household are children
       or adolescents age 17 or younger?                        ( , )_ _ Number of children

   c.  Are you  READ RESPONSES                                  ( ) 1 Married and living with
                                                                       your husband/wife
                                                                     2 Separated (for reasons
                                                                       other than hospital-
                                                                       ization, military
                                                                       service, etc.)
                                                                     3 Divorced
                                                                     4 Widowed
                                                                     5 Never married
                                                                     6 Married but temporarily
                                                                       separated (hospital-
                                                                       ization, military
                                                                       service, etc.)
                                                                     7 Other (specify) _____

---

ASK ONLY AT INTAKE

5.  What is your race?                                          ( ) 1 White, not Spanish
                                                                       descent
                                                                     2 White, Spanish origin
                                                                       or descent
                                                                     3 Black
                                                                     4 Native American
                                                                       (Indian)
                                                                     5 Chinese
                                                                     6 Japanese
                                                                     7 Other (specify)_____

6.  What is the last grade in school or college that you have   ( ) 1 Less than 6 years of
    completed?                                                          schooling
                                                                     2 Completed 6th, 7th,
                                                                       8th, 9th, 10th or
                                                                       11th grades
                                                                     3 Graduated from high
                                                                       school
                                                                     4 Some college or
                                                                       technical school
                                                                     5 Graduated from college
                                                                     6 Special education for
                                                                       the exceptional--
                                                                       ungraded school
                                                                     7 Other (specify) _____

BACKGROUND INFORMATION, CONT'D.

-------------------------------------------------------------------------------------------------

7.  What problem or problems led you to come for help at the Social
    Services Department; what kind of help do you/did you want?

INTERVIEWER:  PLEASE PROBE FOR ADDITIONAL RESPONSES         RESPONSES WILL BE CODED BY COORDINATOR OR ANALYST

    _____         ( , , )_ _ _Problem Code
    _____         ( , , )_ _ _Problem Code
    _____         ( , , )_ _ _Problem Code
    _____         ( , , )_ _ _Problem Code

ASK ONLY AT FOLLOW-UP

7b.  Do you still have this problem/these problems?  Is it/are they  READ RESPONSES          (  ) 1 Entirely gone or much
                                                                                                  better
         Details: _____                                     2 Somewhat better
                  _____                                     3 Still the same
                                                                                               4 Somewhat worse ⎰ ASK FOR
                                                                                               5 Much worse      ⎱ DETAILS

| CLIENT SATISFACTION | | ( , , )_ _ _ _ Client I.D. |
|---|---|---|
| | | ( ) ② Follow-up |
| | | ( ) ① Questionnaire Version |
| | | ( , ) ⑫ Module Number |

ASK ONLY AT FOLLOW-UP

8. I am going to read you a list of services that the records show you have received from the Social Services Department since we last interviewed you in _____ (month and year of pre-service interview). We would like to know how satisfied you were with each service. How satisfied have you been with the ...

READ NAME OF EACH SERVICE AND ANSWER CHOICES. IF CLIENT ANSWERS "SOMEWHAT DISSATISFIED" OR "VERY DISSATISFIED," ASK FOR DETAILS --e.g., "Can you tell me something about what the problem was with the service?"

COORDINATOR WILL FILL IN SERVICE CODES

| | Very satisfied | Somewhat satisfied | No feelings one way or the other | Somewhat dissatisfied | Very dissatisfied | Thinks did not get this service | |
|---|---|---|---|---|---|---|---|
| a. ..._____ service? Details: _____ _____ | ☐ 1 | ☐ 2 | ☐ 3 | ☐ 4 [ASK FOR DETAILS] | ☐ 5 | ☐ 6 | ( , )_ _ Service Code ( )_ Response |
| b. ..._____ service? Details: _____ _____ | ☐ 1 | ☐ 2 | ☐ 3 | ☐ 4 [ASK FOR DETAILS] | ☐ 5 | ☐ 6 | ( , )_ _ Service Code ( )_ Response |
| c. ..._____ service? Details: _____ _____ | ☐ 1 | ☐ 2 | ☐ 3 | ☐ 4 [ASK FOR DETAILS] | ☐ 5 | ☐ 6 | ( , )_ _ Service Code ( )_ Response |
| d. ..._____ service? Details: _____ _____ | ☐ 1 | ☐ 2 | ☐ 3 | ☐ 4 [ASK FOR DETAILS] | ☐ 5 | ☐ 6 | ( , )_ _ Service Code ( )_ Response |
| e. ..._____ service? Details: _____ _____ | ☐ 1 | ☐ 2 | ☐ 3 | ☐ 4 [ASK FOR DETAILS] | ☐ 5 | ☐ 6 | ( , )_ _ Service Code ( )_ Response |
| f. ..._____ service? Details: _____ _____ | ☐ 1 | ☐ 2 | ☐ 3 | ☐ 4 [ASK FOR DETAILS] | ☐ 5 | ☐ 6 | ( , )_ _ Service Code ( )_ Response |

Are there any other services that you received from the Social Services Department since _____(month and year of pre-service interview) that I have not mentioned?

IF CLIENT NAMES ADDITIONAL SERVICES, RECORD ABOVE AND ASK ABOUT SATISFACTION FOR EACH ADDITIONAL SERVICE.

9. In general, considering all your contacts with the Social Services Department and all the services you received since we first interviewed you, how satisfied do you feel with the Department?

| Details: _____ _____ | ☐ 1 | ☐ 2 | ☐ 3 | ☐ 4 [ASK FOR DETAILS] | ☐ 5 | ( )_ Response |
|---|---|---|---|---|---|---|

10. Since _____ (month and year of pre-service interview), have you received any services from other agencies, from churches, or from other sources besides the Social Services Department?

FOR EACH SERVICE THE CLIENT LISTS, WRITE THE SERVICE AND WHAT AGENCY PROVIDED IT.

COORDINATOR WILL FILL IN SERVICE AND AGENCY CODES

| _____ (service) | from _____ (source) | ( , )_ _ Service Code ( , )_ _ Agency Code |
|---|---|---|
| _____ (service) | from _____ (source) | ( , )_ _ Service Code ( , )_ _ Agency Code |
| _____ (service) | from _____ (source) | ( , )_ _ Service Code ( , )_ _ Agency Code |

CLIENT SATISFICATION CONT'D.

11. Were there any services that you wanted or expected that you did not get?

IF "YES," ASK FOR DETAILS OF WHAT SERVICES AND REASONS WHY CLIENT DID NOT GET THEM.

Service and reasons: _____

Service and reasons: _____

Service and reasons: _____

COORDINATOR WILL FILL IN SERVICE AND AGENCY CODES

( , )_ _ Service Code

( , )_ _ Service Code

( , )_ _ Service Code

12. How many times have you met with social workers in-person, face-to-face, since we first interviewed you? (Do not count times you met with financial eligibility, medicaid or food stamp workers.)

IF CLIENT CANNOT SAY EXACT NUMBER, GET APPROXIMATE NUMBER

( , )_ _ Number of in-person contacts

13. How many times have you talked on the telephone with social workers since we first interviewed you? (Do not count times you met with financial eligibility, medicaid or food stamp workers.)

IF CLIENT CANNOT SAY EXACT NUMBER, GET APPROXIMATE NUMBER

( , )_ _ Number of telephone contacts

DURING THE FOLLOWING QUESTIONS REMIND CLIENT TO CONSIDER ONLY SERVICES, NOT FINANCIAL AID, FOOD STAMPS, OR MEDICAID--e.g. "Remember that during these questions we are asking only about services--(LIST THE SERVICES THE CLIENT RECEIVED)--and not about financial aid, food stamps or medicaid."

14. We are concerned with how long it takes to get services started after clients first apply. I would like you to rate how satisfied you were with how fast you got services after you applied for them. Were you READ RESPONSES

Details: _____

( ) 1 Very satisfied
2 Somewhat satisfied
3 No feelings one way or the other
4 Somewhat dissatisfied ⎫ ASK FOR
5 Very dissatisfied ⎬ DETAILS

15. How satisfied are you with the way people at the Social Services Department treated you--for example, have they been polite and have they paid attention to you? Have you been READ RESPONSES

Details: _____

( ) 1 Very satisfied
2 Somewhat satisfied
3 No feelings one way or the other
4 Somewhat dissatisfied ⎫ ASK FOR
5 Very dissatisfied ⎬ DETAILS

16. How satisfied are you with the location of the Social Services Department office--is it easy for you to get to? Are you READ RESPONSES

Details: _____

( ) 1 Very satisfied
2 Somewhat satisfied
3 No feelings one way or the other
4 Somewhat dissatisfied ⎫ ASK FOR
5 Very dissatisfied ⎬ DETAILS

17. How easy or difficult has it been to get in touch with your social workers when you needed to talk with them or see them--do they return your calls promptly or see you right away? Have you been READ RESPONSES

Details: _____

( ) 1 Very satisfied
2 Somewhat satisfied
3 No feelings one way or the other
4 Somewhat dissatisfied ⎫ ASK FOR
5 Very dissatisfied ⎬ DETAILS

18. Overall, would you say your problems are better, worse, or the same as they were in _____ (month and year of pre-service interview) when we first interviewed you? Are things READ RESPONSES

Details: _____

( ) 1 Much better
2 Somewhat better
3 About the same
4 Somewhat worse ⎫ ASK FOR
5 Much worse ⎬ DETAILS

19. Overall, do you feel that the services you received from the Social Services Department had any effect--good or bad--on your problems?

Details: _____

( ) 1 A good effect ASK WHICH SERVICES
2 No effect (or got no help)
3 A bad effect ⎫ ASK FOR
4 Good and bad effects ⎬ DETAILS

| PHYSICAL HEALTH | ( , , , )_ _ _ _ Client I.D. |

( ) 1 Intake
     2 Follow-up

( ) (1) Questionnaire Version

( , ) (03) Module Number

The next few questions ask about your physical health.

20. During the past month, how many days were you so sick that you could not do the things you usually do?

( ) 1 0-2 days
     2 3-7 days
     3 8-14 days
     4 More than 14 days

---

21. How would you rate your physical health in the past month? READ RESPONSE

( ) 1 Excellent
     2 Good
     3 Fair
     4 Poor

---

22. In the past month, have health troubles stood in the way of your doing the things you wanted to do? Were there READ RESPONSES

( ) 1 No problems
     2 Minor problems
     3 Medium problems
     4 Major problems

---

23. In the past month, did you have problems getting medical care when you needed it? Were there READ RESPONSES

( ) 1 No problems or did not need medical care
     2 Minor problems
     3 Medium problems   ASK FOR DETAILS
     4 Major problems

ANALYST WILL CODE

Details: _____

( , )_ _ Nature of problems

---

| ASK ONLY AT FOLLOW-UP |

24. When you compare your physical health now to what it was like when we first interviewed you, would you say it is now READ RESPONSES

( ) 1 Much better
     2 Somewhat better
     3 About the same
     4 Somewhat worse
     5 Much worse
     6 No problems then or now

| PERFORMANCE OF ACTIVITIES OF DAILY LIVING | ( , , , )_ _ _ _ Client I.D. |

( ) 1 Intake
  2 Follow-up

( ) ① Questionnaire Version
( , )④ Module Number

---

IF CLIENT IS 17 OR YOUNGER, SKIP TO Q. 30

Now I want to ask you some questions about any difficulties you may have in doing your day-to-day chores.

25. In the past month, have you had any disabilities or illnesses which made it difficult for you to do cooking, housework, shopping or laundry?

( ) 1 No- ASK a

2 Yes- SKIP TO Q. 26

   a. Does someone else usually do these chores for you? IF YES
      Could you do these chores yourself if you had to?

( ) 1 No one else does chores

2 Someone else does chores but client could do them himself — SKIP TO Q.30

IF THE CLIENT HAS DIFFICULTY OR IF SOMEONE ELSE DID THESE CHORES AND THE CLIENT COULD NOT DO THE CHORES BY HIMSELF OR HERSELF, CONTINUE WITH Q. 26. IF CLIENT HAS OR WOULD HAVE NO DIFFICULTY, SKIP TO Q. 30.

3 Someone else does chores and client could not do them himself/herself — CONTINUE WITH Q.26

---

The next questions ask about these chores one-by-one.

26. a. In the past month, have you had any difficulty doing your own cooking by yourself? Have you had READ RESPONSES

( ) 1 No problems
2 Minor problems
3 Medium problems
4 Major problems

   b. In the past month, did anyone help you with cooking? Who helped?

( ) 1 No one
2 Friend or relative
3 Agency homemaker or chore worker
4 Other (specify) _____

   c. Considering any help you have had with cooking, in addition to your own efforts, how satisfied have you been with how well the cooking gets done? Have you been READ RESPONSES

( ) 1 Very satisfied
2 Somewhat satisfied
3 No feelings one way or the other
4 Somewhat dissatisfied
5 Very dissatisfied

---

27. a. In the past month, have you had any difficulty doing your own housework by yourself? Have you had READ RESPONSES

( ) 1 No problems
2 Minor problems
3 Medium problems
4 Major problems

   b. In the past month, did anyone help you with housework? Who helped?

( ) 1 No one
2 Friend or relative
3 Agency homemaker or chore worker
4 Other (specify) _____

   c. Considering any help you have had with housework, in addition to your own efforts, how satisfied have you been with how well the housework gets done? Have you been READ RESPONSES

( ) 1 Very satisfied
2 Somewhat satisfied
3 No feelings one way or the other
4 Somewhat dissatisfied
5 Very dissatisfied

---

PERFORMANCE OF ACTIVITIES
OF DAILY LIVING, CONT'D.

28.  a.  In the past month, have you had any difficulty doing your own
shopping for things like groceries or clothes by yourself?
Have you had READ RESPONSES

( )  1 No problems
2 Minor problems
3 Medium problems
4 Major problems

b.  In the past month, did anyone help you with shopping?  Who helped?

( )  1 No one
2 Friend or relative
3 Agency homemaker or
chore worker
4 Other (specify) _____

c.  Considering any help you have had with shopping, in addition to
your own efforts, how satisfied have you been with how well the
shopping gets done?  Have you been READ RESPONSES

( )  1 Very satisfied
2 Somewhat satisfied
3 No feelings one way
or the other
4 Somewhat dissatisfied
5 Very dissatisfied

29.  a.  In the past month, have you had any difficulty doing your own
laundry by yourself?  Have you had READ RESPONSES

( )  1 No problems
2 Minor problems
3 Medium problems
4 Major problems

b.  In the past month, did anyone help you with your laundry?  Who helped?

( )  1 No one
2 Friend or relative
3 Agency homemaker or
chore worker
4 Other (specify) _____

c.  Considering any help you have had with your laundry, in addition to
your own efforts, how satisfied have you been with how well the
laundry gets done?  Have you been READ RESPONSES

( )  1 Very satisfied
2 Somewhat satisfied
3 No feelings one way
or the other
4 Somewhat dissatisfied
5 Very dissatisfied

30.  In the past month, have you had any disabilities or illnesses that made it
difficult for you to feed yourself, take baths, wash your hair yourself,
or take medicine?

( )  1 No- SKIP TO Q.35
2 Yes- CONTINUE WITH Q.31

31.  a.  In the past month, have you had any difficulty feeding yourself?
Have you had READ RESPONSES

( )  1 No problems
2 Minor problems
3 Medium problems
4 Major problems

b.  In the past month, did anyone help you with feeding yourself?  Who helped?

( )  1 No one
2 Friend or relative
3 Agency homemaker or
chore worker
4 Other (specify) _____

c.  Considering any help you have had with feeding yourself, in addition to
your own efforts, how satisfied have you been with the way you manage
feeding yourself?  Have you been READ RESPONSES

( )  1 Very satisfied
2 Somewhat satisfied
3 No feelings one way
or the other
4 Somewhat dissatisfied
5 Very dissatisfied

32.  a.  In the past month, have you had any difficulty taking baths or showers,
or washing your hair by yourself?  Have you had READ RESPONSES

( )  1 No problems
2 Minor problems
3 Medium problems
4 Major problems

b.  In the past month, did anyone help you with bathing yourself, or
washing your hair?  Who helped?

( )  1 No one
2 Friend or relative
3 Agency homemaker or
chore worker
4 Other (specify) _____

c.  Considering any help you have had with bathing yourself, or washing
your hair, in addition to your own efforts, how satisfied
have you been with the way you manage bathing yourself and washing
your hair?  Have you been READ RESPONSES

( )  1 Very satisfied
2 Somewhat satisfied
3 No feelings one way
or the other
4 Somewhat dissatisfied
5 Very dissatisfied

PERFORMANCE OF ACTIVITIES
OF DAILY LIVING, CONT'D.

---

33. a. In the past month, have you had any difficulty getting to the bathroom and using the toilet by yourself? Have you had [ READ RESPONSES ]

( ) 1 No problems
2 Minor problems
3 Medium problems
4 Major problems

b. In the past month, did anyone help you with getting to the bathroom and using the toilet? Who helped? [ READ RESPONSES ]

( ) 1 No one
2 Friend or relative
3 Agency homemaker or chore worker
4 Other (specify) _____

c. Considering any help you have had with getting to the bathroom and using the toilet, in addition to your own efforts, how satisfied have you been with the way you manage getting to the bathroom and using the toilet? Have you been [ READ RESPONSES ]

( ) 1 Very satisfied
2 Somewhat satisfied
3 No feelings one way or the other
4 Somewhat dissatisfied
5 Very dissatisfied

---

34. a. In the past month, have you had any difficulty taking your medicine by yourself? Have you had [ READ RESPONSES ]

( ) 1 No problems
2 Minor problems
3 Medium problems
4 Major problems

b. In the past month, did anyone help you to take your medicine? Who helped? READ RESPONSES

( ) 1 No one
2 Friend or relative
3 Agency homemaker or chore worker
4 Other (specify) _____

c. Considering any help you have had with taking your medicine, in addition to your own efforts, how satisfied have you been with the way you manage to take your medicine? Have you been [ READ RESPONSES ]

( ) 1 Very satisfied
2 Somewhat satisfied
3 No feelings one way or the other
4 Somewhat dissatisfied
5 Very dissatisfied

---

35. a. In the past month, have you had any difficulty getting around by yourself? Have you had [ READ RESPONSES ]

( ) 1 No problems
2 Minor problems
3 Medium problems
4 Major problems

b. In the past month, did anyone help you to get around? Who helped? [ READ RESPONSES ]

( ) 1 No one
2 Friend or relative
3 Agency homemaker or chore worker
4 Other (specify) _____

c. Considering any help you have had getting around, in addition to your own efforts, how satisfied have you been with the way you manage to get around? Have you been [ READ RESPONSES ]

( ) 1 Very satisfied
2 Somewhat satisfied
3 No feelings one way or the other
4 Somewhat dissatisfied
5 Very dissatisfied

---

36. a. In the past month, have you had any difficulty getting to places beyond walking distance? Have you had [ READ RESPONSES ]

( ) 1 No problems
2 Minor problems
3 Medium problems
4 Major problems

b. In the past month, did anyone help you to get to places beyond walking distance? Who helped? [ READ RESPONSES ]

( ) 1 No one
2 Friend or relative
3 Agency homemaker or chore worker
4 Other (specify) _____

c. Considering any help you have had getting to places beyond walking distance, in addition to your own efforts, how satisfied have you been with the way you manage to get to places beyond walking distance? [ READ RESPONSES ]

( ) 1 Very satisfied
2 Somewhat satisfied
3 No feelings one way or the other
4 Somewhat dissatisfied
5 Very dissatisfied

---

PERFORMANCE OF ACTIVITIES
OF DAILY LIVING, CONT'D.

ASK ONLY AT FOLLOW-UP

37.   Now think about whether you had any problems with taking care of
      yourself or doing everyday activities when we first interviewed
      you in _____ (month and year of pre-service interview).
      ( PAUSE )   When you compare then and now, would you say things
      now are   READ RESPONSE

( )   1 Much better
      2 Somewhat better
      3 About the same
      4 Somewhat worse
      5 Much worse
      6 No problem then or now

| MENTAL DISTRESS | | ( , , , )_ _ _ Client I.D. |
|---|---|---|

( )1 Intake
  2 Follow-up
( X1) Questionnaire Version
( , )05 Module Number

Now I would like to ask a few questions about how you have been feeling
during the past month.

38. In the past month, how often have you felt <u>fearful</u> or <u>afraid</u>?
    READ RESPONSES

( )1 Never
  2 Once or twice
  3 Often
  4 Almost always

39. <u>In the past month</u>, how often have you felt <u>sad</u> or <u>depressed</u>? READ RESPONSES

( )1 Never
  2 Once or twice
  3 Often
  4 Almost always

40. In the past month, how often have you felt <u>angry</u>? READ RESPONSES

( )1 Never
  2 Once or twice
  3 Often
  4 Almost always

41. In the past month, how often have you felt <u>mixed up</u> or <u>confused</u>?
    READ RESPONSES

( )1 Never
  2 Once or twice
  3 Often
  4 Almost always

42. <u>In the past month</u>, how often have you felt <u>nervous</u> or <u>worried</u>? READ RESPONSES

( )1 Never
  2 Once or twice
  3 Often
  4 Almost always

43. <u>In the past month</u>, have you had trouble <u>sleeping</u>? READ RESPONSES

( )1 Never
  2 Once or twice
  3 Often
  4 Almost always

44. <u>In the past month</u>, have you had trouble with <u>headaches</u>? READ RESPONSES

( )1 Never
  2 Once or twice
  3 Often
  4 Almost always

45. <u>In the past month</u>, have you had trouble with <u>poor appetite</u>? READ RESPONSES

( )1 Never
  2 Once or twice
  3 Often
  4 Almost always

46. <u>In the past month</u>, have you had <u>trouble with an upset stomach</u>? READ RESPONSES

( )1 Never
  2 Once or twice
  3 Often
  4 Almost always

47. In the past month, have you had trouble with <u>feeling very tired</u>?
    READ RESPONSES

( )1 Never
  2 Once or twice
  3 Often
  4 Almost always

COORDINATOR: ADD SCORES
FOR QUESTIONS 38-47

( , )_ _Symptom Distress Score

MENTAL DISTRESS CONT'D.

---

48.  In the past month, did you find yourself feeling quite lonely?

READ RESPONSES

(  )1 Never
2 Once or twice
3 Often
4 Almost always

---

49.  In the past month, how often did you feel you did not want to go on living?

READ RESPONSES

(  )1 Never
2 Once or twice
3 Often
4 Almost always

---

ASK ONLY AT FOLLOW-UP

50.  When you compare your mental and emotional health now to what it was like when we first interviewed you, would you say it is now  READ RESPONSES

(  )1 Much better
2 Somewhat better
3 About the same
4 Somewhat worse
5 Much worse
6 No problems then or now

FAMILY STRENGTH

( , , )_ _ _ _Client I.D.
( )1 Intake
  2 Follow-up
( )① Questionnaire Version
( , )06 Module Number

---

IF CLIENT LIVES IN AN INSTITUTION, OR GROUP RESIDENCE (NOT A FOSTER HOME), SKIP TO Q. 55

Now I am going to ask you some questions about how you and your family and friends get along together.

IF CLIENT LIVES ALONE, SKIP TO Q. 54

51. In the past month, have you and the people you live with had problems handling arguments and working out differences? Would you say there were READ RESPONSES

( )1 No problems
  2 Minor problems
  3 Medium problems
  4 Major problems

---

52. In the past month, have the people you live with had problems feeling close to each other? Would you say there were READ RESPONSES

( )1 No problems
  2 Minor problems
  3 Medium problems
  4 Major problems

---

53. In the past month, have there been problems related to drug or alcohol abuse by another adult or child in the household? Would you say there READ RESPONSES

( )1 No problems
  2 Minor problems
  3 Medium problems
  4 Major problems
  0 Not applicable--only client and small children (age 0-10) in household

---

IF CLIENT IS IN FOSTER CARE OR A GROUP HOME, SKIP TO Q. 55

54. In the past month, have you had any problems with family or close friends who do not live with you? Have you seen them as often as you wanted to, and have you gotten along well together? Would you say there were READ RESPONSES

SKIP TO Q. 61

( )1 No problems
  2 Minor problems
  3 Medium problems  SKIP TO Q. 61
  4 Major problems

---

ASK Qs. 55-60 ONLY OF CLIENTS LIVING IN SUBSTITUTE CARE (FOSTER CARE, GROUP HOME, OR INSTITUTION)

55. ASK ONLY OF ADOLESCENTS

Do you have any contact with your parents, brothers or sisters? IF YES In the past month, have you seen or talked to your parents, brothers or sisters as often as you wanted to?

( )1 Contact, as often as wanted to
  2 Contact, not as often as wanted to
  3 No contact
  0 Not applicable--no parents, brothers or sisters

FAMILY STRENGTH, CONT'D.

---

56. Are you married or do you have children? | IF YES | In the past month, have you seen or talked to your husband/wife and/or children as often as you wanted to?

( )1 As often as wanted to
2 Not as often as wanted to
0 Not applicable--not married and no children

---

57. Do you have any other relatives or close friends who visit you here or whom you go out to visit? | IF YES | In the past month, have there been as many visits with them as you would like?

( )1 Contact, enough visits
2 Contact, not enough visits
3 No contacts

IF CLIENT IS IN FOSTER CARE, SKIP TO Q. 61

---

ASK Qs. 58-60 ONLY OF CLIENTS WHO LIVE IN AN INSTITUTION OR GROUP RESIDENCE

58. Do you have any close friends among the staff or other people who live here (in the group residence/institution)?

( )1 Yes
2 No
0 Not applicable, just arrived at institution

---

59. In the past month, have you and the people who are important to you (both "inside" and "outside") had trouble handling arguments and working out differences? Would you say there were | READ RESPONSES |

( )1 No problems
2 Minor problems
3 Medium problems
4 Major problems
5 No one important to them

---

60. In the past month, have you and the people who are important to you had trouble feeling close to each other? Would you say there were | READ RESPONSES |

( )1 No problems
2 Minor problems
3 Medium problems
4 Major problems
5 No one important to them

ASK ONLY AT FOLLOW-UP

61. Overall, when you compare how you and your family, friends, and relatives get along together now with how you and they got along when we first interviewed you, would you say things are now | READ RESPONSES |

( )1 Much better
2 Somewhat better
3 About the same
4 Somewhat worse
5 Much worse
6 No problems then or now

| QUALITY OF SUBSTITUTE CARE | ( , , , )_ _ _Client I.D. |
|---|---|
| | ( )1 Intake |
| | 2 Follow-up |
| | ( X) Questionnaire Version |
| | ( , )07 Module Number |

---

INTERVIEWER: THIS SECTION APPLIES ONLY IF CLIENT HAS BEEN IN AN INSTITUTION, IN GROUP RESIDENTIAL PLACEMENT OR IN FOSTER CARE FOR THE PAST TWO WEEKS. IF CLIENT LIVES IN OWN HOME, SKIP TO CHILD PROBLEM BEHAVIOR MODULE, Q. 100.

The next questions are about conditions in the place where you live.

62. In the past two weeks, have you been satisfied with the food (temperature, taste, amount)? Have you been [ READ RESPONSES ]
( )1 Very satisfied
2 Satisfied
3 Dissatisfied
4 Very dissatisfied

---

63. In the past two weeks, have you been satisfied with how often you got clean sheets and towels? Have you been [ READ RESPONSES ]
( )1 Very satisfied
2 Satisfied
3 Dissatisfied
4 Very dissatisfied

---

64. In the past two weeks, have you been satisfied that there are enough opportunities for visits from your outside friends and relatives--for example, was there a good place to talk with your visitors, were they welcome to visit, and so on? Have you been [ READ RESPONSES ]
( )1 Very satisfied
2 Satisfied
3 Dissatisfied
4 Very dissatisfied

---

65. In the past two weeks, have you had enough clean clothes? Have you been [ READ RESPONSES ]
( )1 Very satisfied
2 Satisfied
3 Dissatisfied
4 Very dissatisfied

---

66. In the past two weeks, how satisfied have you been with the recreational activities offered here? [ READ RESPONSES ]
( )1 Very satisfied
2 Satisfied
3 Dissatisfied
4 Very dissatisfied

---

67. In the past two weeks, have the staff/the foster family members been helpful and did they treat you well? Have you been [ READ RESPONSES ]
( )1 Very satisfied
2 Satisfied
3 Dissatisfied
4 Very dissatisfied

---

68. In the past two weeks, has the temperature of your room been comfortable? Have you been [ READ RESPONSES ]
( )1 Very satisfied
2 Satisfied
3 Dissatisfied
4 Very dissatisfied

---

69. Is there someone to whom you can make an official complaint about something you do not like here?
( )1 No
2 Yes
3 Do not know

---

70. In the past year, have you made an official complaint about the place where you are living now?
( )1 Yes
2 No [ SKIP TO Q. 77 ]

a. How satisfied were you with how your complaint was handled? Were you [ READ RESPONSES ]
( )1 Very satisfied
2 Satisfied
3 Dissatisfied
4 Very dissatisfied

---

71. In the past two weeks, have you liked the way the place looked (appearance, cleanness, general maintenance)? Have you been [ READ RESPONSES ]
( )1 Very satisfied
2 Satisfied
3 Dissatisfied
4 Very dissatisfied

---

72. During the past two weeks, have you felt that your personal things are kept safe so that no could take them or damage them? Have you been [ READ RESPONSES ]
( )1 Very satisfied
2 Satisfied
3 Dissatisfied
4 Very dissatisfied

---

73. Overall, which of the following statements best describes how you feel about the place where you are now living? [ READ RESPONSES ]
( )1 Very satisfied
2 Satisfied
3 Dissatisfied
4 Very dissatisfied

---

| ASK ONLY AT FOLLOW-UP |
|---|

74. When you compare conditions where you live now to conditions in your home when we first interviewed you, would you say that they are now [ READ RESPONSES ]
( )1 Much better
2 Somewhat better
3 About the same
4 Somewhat worse
5 Much worse
6 No problems then or now

CHILD BEHAVIOR AND PARENTING

( , , , ) _ _ _ _ Client I.D.

( ) 1 Intake
    2 Follow-up

( ) ①Questionnaire Version

( , ) ⑱ Module Number

---

IF RESPONDENT IS AN ADULT (18 OR OVER) AND THERE ARE NO CHILDREN
(AGE 17 OR UNDER) IN HOUSEHOLD, SKIP TO ALCOHOL AND DRUG ABUSE
MODULE. IF RESPONDENT IS AGE 14 TO 17, SKIP TO Q. 85.

I have asked a few general questions about your family and the child(ren)
in your household. The following questions ask about specific difficulties
some parents and children have.

75. a. How many children do you have in your household who are age 4 or
    younger?

    ( , )_ _ Number of children
    age 0-4

ASK Q. 75b IF CLIENT HAS CHILD(REN)
AGE 0-4; IF NOT, SKIP TO Q.76

  b. In the past month, have you been at all concerned with the way the
    child(ren) age 4 and under are developing or behaving compared to
    other children their age? Were there READ RESPONSES

    ( )1 No problems
    2 Minor problems
    3 Medium problems
    4 Major problems

---

76. a. How many children do you have in your household who are 5-17
    years old?

    ( )_ _ Number of children
    age 5-17

CONTINUE WITH Q. 76b IF CLIENT HAS CHILD(REN)
AGE 5-17; IF NOT SKIP TO Q. 94

  b. In the past month, did the child/any of the children have tantrums or fight
    with other children? Were there READ RESPONSES

    ( )1 No problems
    2 Minor probems
    3 Medium problems
    4 Major problems

---

77. In the past month, did the child/any of the children lie or act
rude or uncooperative? Were there READ RESPONSES

    ( )1 No problems
    2 Minor problems
    3 Medium problems
    4 Major problems

---

78. In the past month, have adults in the household had problems with
disciplining or training the children? Were there READ RESPONSES

    ( )1 No problems
    2 Minor problems
    3 Medium problems
    4 Major problems

---

79. DELETED

CHILD BEHAVIOR AND PARENTING

80. In the past month, did the child/any of the children steal or destroy property? Were there READ RESPONSES

( )1 No problems
2 Minor problems
3 Medium problems
4 Major problems

81. In the past year, how many of the children have been in school?

_ _ Number of children in school IF 0 SKIP TO Q.82

a. In the past six months, did the child/any of the children have school problems (skipping classes, failing courses or having to repeat grades, being suspended or expelled, or dropping out)? Were there READ RESPONSES

( )1 No problems
2 Minor problems
3 Medium problems } Ask
4 Major problems } b

b. What were these problems?

1 Skipped classes
2 Failed a course
3 Failed a grade
4 Suspended or expelled
5 Dropped out
6 Other _____
_____

CHILD BEHAVIOR AND PARENTING, CONT'D.

---

82. In the past month, have you had complaints from neighbors, teachers, police or other people about the child's/any of the children's behavior?  Were there READ RESPONSES

( )1 No problems
2 Minor problems
3 Medium problems
4 Major problems

---

83. a. How many children do you have in your household who are 11-17 years old?

( )_ _ Number of children age 11-17

CONTINUE WITH Q. 84   IF CLIENT HAS CHILD(REN) AGE 11-17; IF NOT, SKIP TO Q. 94.

---

84. In the past month, has the child/have any of the children had problems breaking curfews, coming home late, keeping "bad" company, or running away?  Were there READ RESPONSES

( )1 No problems
2 Minor problems
3 Medium problems
4 Major problems

---

CHILD BEHAVIOR AND PARENTING, CONT'D.

---

QUESTIONS 85 THROUGH 92 SHOULD BE ASKED ONLY IF
RESPONDENT IS AN ADOLESCENT AGED 14 THROUGH 17

85. In the past month, did you have trouble controlling your anger (getting into fights, losing your temper, breaking or damaging things)? Were there READ RESPONSES

( )1 No problems
2 Minor problems
3 Medium problems
4 Major problems

---

86. In the past month, did you have conflicts with school authorities, police or other adults? Were there READ RESPONSES

( )1 No problems
2 Minor problems
3 Medium problems
4 Major problems

---

87. Are you presently enrolled in school?

No ASK a THEN SKIP TO Q. 90

Yes SKIP TO Q. 88

a. Why is that? Please explain.
READ RESPONSES

( )1 Not in school because of illness, vacation, or having graduated.
2 Dropped out
3 Other reason (specify): ____

---

88. In the past month, how often did you skip school without permission? READ RESPONSES

( )1 Never
2 Once
3 Two or three times
4 Four or more times

---

89. In the past month, how would you rate your school performance? READ RESPONSES

( )1 Excellent
2 Good
3 Fair
4 Poor

---

90. In the past month, were your parents worried about your keeping "bad" company READ RESPONSES

( )1 No
2 Yes

a. Do you think you have been keeping "bad" company?

( )1 No
2 Yes

---

91. In the past month, how often have you broken curfews, come home late? READ RESPONSES

( )1 Never
2 Once
3 Two or three times
4 Four or more times

CHILD BEHAVIOR AND PARENTING, CONT'D.

ASK ONLY AT FOLLOW-UP

92. Now think about whether you had such difficulties when we first interviewed you. (PAUSE) When you compare then and now, would you say things now are [ READ RESPONSES ]

( )1 Much better
2 Somewhat better
3 About the same
4 Somewhat worse
5 Much worse
6 No problems then or now

INTERVIEWER: IF ADOLESCENT (AGE 14-17) HAS OWN CHILD LIVING IN THE SAME HOUSEHOLD, ASK Q. 93 and 94; OTHERWISE SKIP TO Q. 95.

93. In the past month, were there problems with the way your child(ren) developed or behaved compared to other children the same age? Were there [ READ RESPONSES ]

( )1 No problems
2 Minor problems
3 Medium problems
4 Major problems
} [ ASK a ]

a. Please explain

INTERVIEWER: PLEASE PROBE FOR ADDITIONAL RESPONSES

_____

_____

ASK ONLY AT FOLLOW-UP

94. Now think about whether there were any problems with the child(ren)'s behavior when we first interviewed you (PAUSE). When you compare then and now, would you say things now are [ READ RESPONSES ]

( )1 Much better
2 Somewhat better
3 About the same
4 Somewhat worse
5 Much worse
6 No problems then or now

ALCOHOL AND DRUG ABUSE

( , , , )_ _ _ Client I.D.

( ) 1 Intake
    2 Follow-up

( ) ① Questionnaire Version

( , ) 09 Module Number

We are asking everyone a set of questions regarding drug and alcohol use.

95. Have you had beverages containing alcohol, whether it was wine, beer, whiskey or some other drink, in the past month?

( ) 1 No    SKIP TO Q. 105
    2 Yes

96. In the past month, about how often would you say you had 5 or more drinks in a day, whether it was beer, wine or whiskey?
READ RESPONSES, STOP AT FIRST YES

( ) 1 Never
    2 Less than once a week
    3 1-2 times a week
    4 3-4 times a week
    5 5 or more times a week, that is, nearly every day

INTERVIEWER: 5 drinks = More than 6 oz. of liquor (more than ¼ pint)
= More than a 6-pack or 2 qts. of beer
= More than a fifth of table wine
= More than 12 oz. of sherry or port (more than 3/4 pint)

97. a. In the past month, have you felt you ought to cut down?
( ) 1 No
    2 Yes

b. In the past month, have people annoyed you by criticizing your drinking?
( ) 1 No
    2 Yes

c. In the past month, have you felt bad or guilty about your drinking?
( ) 1 No
    2 Yes

d. In the past month, have you had to have a drink first thing in the morning to steady your nerves or get rid of a hangover?
( ) 1 No
    2 Yes

COORDINATOR: RECORD HOW MANY OF Q. 97a-d WERE ANSWERED "YES"
( ) 1 0
    2 1
    3 2
    4 3
    5 4

ASK Q. 98 AND 99 ONLY OF ADOLESCENTS (AGE 17 AND YOUNGER)

98. In the past month, did you drink more than most of your friends?
( ) 1 No
    2 Yes

ALCOHOL AND DRUG ABUSE, CONT'D.

---

ASK ONLY OF ADOLESCENTS

99.  In the past month, did you ever drink for the following reasons:

    a.  Because you were bored?

      ( ) 1 No
          2 Yes  ASK HOW OFTEN

       How often did you drink because you were bored?  READ RESPONSES

      ( ) 1 Once or twice
          2 3 to 5 times
          3 6 or more times

    b.  Because you were angry?

      ( ) 1 No
          2 Yes  ASK HOW OFTEN

       How often did you drink because you were angry?  READ RESPONSES

      ( ) 1 Once or twice
          2 3 to 5 times
          3 6 or more times

    c.  Because you were nervous or worried?

      ( ) 1 No
          2 Yes  ASK HOW OFTEN

       How often did you drink because you were nervous or worried?  READ RESPONSES

      ( ) 1 Once or twice
          2 3 to 5 times
          3 6 or more times

    d.  To get drunk?

      ( ) 1 No
          2 Yes  ASK HOW OFTEN

       How often did you drink to get drunk?  READ RESPONSES

      ( ) 1 Once or twice
          2 3 to 5 times
          3 6 or more times

---

100. In the past month, has your drinking caused any problems with the things you have to do (working at your job or around the house, finding or keeping a job, going to school, and so on)?  Were there  READ RESPONSES

    ( ) 1 No problems
        2 Minor problems
        3 Medium problems
        4 Major problems

---

101. In the past month, has your drinking caused any problem or conflict with your family or friends?  Were there  READ RESPONSES

    ( ) 1 No problems
        2 Minor problems
        3 Medium problems
        4 Major problems

---

102. In the past month, have you had problems after drinking such as being in accidents or fights?  Were there  READ RESPONSES

    ( ) 1 No problems
        2 Minor problems
        3 Medium problems
        4 Major problems

---

103. In the past month, have you been arrested during or following a drinking episode (for instance, for public drunkenness, driving under the influence or disorderly conduct)?

    ( ) 1 No
        2 Yes

---

104. Do you feel alcohol is a problem for you?

    ( ) 1 No  GO TO Q. 105
        2 I'm not sure
        3 Yes  } ASK a

    a.  Are you getting any help for the problem?  Please explain:

      INTERVIEWER:  PLEASE PROBE FOR ADDITIONAL RESPONSES

      _____

      _____

      _____

      _____

      _____

      _____

      _____

( ) 1 Getting help (Alcoholics Anonymous, private clinic, etc.)
     2 Looking for help, but does not know where to find it
     3 Does not feel needs help
     4 Received help, but feels it did no good
     5 Received help and no longer needs it
     6 Not sure what to do about it
     7 Other (specify) _____

ALCOHOL AND DRUG ABUSE, CONT'D.

105. <u>In the past month</u>, did you use any of the following drugs without a prescription: marijuana, cocain, psychedelics, downers, uppers, opiates, or other drugs?

( ) 1 No
    2 Yes     ASK WHAT DRUGS AND HOW OFTEN

Which drugs?

    a. _____

       How often?

( ) 1 Never
    2 Less than once a week
    3 1-2 times a week
    4 3-4 times a week
    5 5 or more times a week, that is, nearly every day

    b. _____

       How often?

( ) 1 Never
    2 Less than once a week
    3 1-2 times a week
    4 3-4 times a week
    5 5 or more times a week, that is, nearly every day

    c. _____

       How often?

( ) 1 Never
    2 Less than once a week
    3 1-2 times a week
    4 3-4 times a week
    5 5 or more times a week, that is, nearly every day

IF CLIENT USES NO DRUGS, SKIP TO Q. <u>112</u>

---

106. Have these drugs caused any problems in your emotional or physical health in the past month? Were there READ RESPONSES

( ) 1 No problems
    2 Minor problems
    3 Medium problems
    4 Major problems

---

107. <u>In the past month</u>, has your use of drugs caused any problem with the things you have to do (working at your job or around the house, finding or keeping a job, going to school, and so on)? Were there READ RESPONSES

( ) 1 Minor problems
    2 Minor problems
    3 Medium problems
    4 Major problems

---

108. Did these drugs cause any problem or conflict with your family or friends <u>in the past month</u>? Were there READ RESPONSES

( ) 1 No problems
    2 Minor problems
    3 Medium problems
    4 Major problems

---

ALCOHOL AND DRUG ABUSE, CONT'D.

---

109. In the past month, have you had problems while on drugs such as accidents or fights? READ RESPONSES

( ) 1 No problems
2 Minor problems
3 Moderate problems
4 Major problems

---

110. In the past month, have you been arrested for possession or use of drugs or driving under the influence of drugs?

( ) 1 No
2 Yes

---

111. Do you feel that you have a drug problem?

( ) 1 No ⎤ SKIP TO ABUSE MODULE, Q. 113
2 I'm not sure ⎫ ASK a
3 Yes ⎭

   a. Are you getting help for the problem? Please explain:

ANALYST WILL CODE

INTERVIEWER: PLEASE PROBE FOR ADDITIONAL RESPONSES

_____

_____

_____

_____

_____

( ) 1 Getting help (Synanon, private clinic, etc.)
2 Looking for help but does not know where to find it
3 Does not feel needs help
4 Received help but feels it did no good
5 Received help and no longer needs it
6 Not sure what to do about it
7 Other (specify) _____

---

ASK ONLY AT FOLLOW-UP

112. Now think about whether you had any problems with drinking when we first interviewed you. (PAUSE) When you compare then and now, would you say things are now READ RESPONSES

( ) 1 Much better
2 Somewhat better
3 About the same
4 Somewhat worse
5 Much worse
6 No problems then or now

---

112A. Think about whether you had any problems with drugs when we first interviewed you. (PAUSE) When you compare then and now, would you say things are now READ RESPONSE

( ) 1 Much better
2 Somewhat better
3 About the same
4 Somewhat worse
5 Much worse
6 No problems then or now

ABUSE

( , , , )_ _ _ _Client I.D.

( ) 1 Intake

2 Follow-up

( ) ①Questionnaire Version

( , )⑩ Module Number

We are asking everyone the following questions regarding abuse.

113.   In the past six months, have you been beaten, or assaulted?

( ) 1 No   SKIP TO Q. 114

2 Yes   ASK a&b

a.  By whom?   READ RESPONSES

IF MORE THAN ONE PERSON ABUSED CLIENT,
CODE 5 AND GIVE DETAILS.

( ) 1 Spouse
2 Parent (or stepparent or
   foster parent)
3 Other relative or friend,
   or acquaintance
4 Stranger (mugged in street,
   etc.)
5 Other (specify) _____

_____

b.  Was it bad enough that you needed medical care?

( ) 1 No
2 Yes

114.   In the past six months, has anyone else in your household, including
the children, been beaten, or assaulted?

( ) 1 No   SKIP TO ECONOMIC SELF
           SUPPORT MODULE

2 Yes   ASK a,b, and c

a.  Who was beaten?   READ RESPONSES

( ) 1 Child age 17 or under
2 Adult age 18 or older

b.  By whom?   READ RESPONSES

( ) 1 Spouse
2 Parent (or stepparent or
   foster parent)
3 Other relative or friend,
   or acquaintance
4 Stranger (mugged in street,
   etc.)
5 Other (specify) _____

_____

c.  Was it bad enough that medical care was needed?

( ) 1 No
2 Yes

ASK ONLY AT FOLLOW-UP

115.   Now think about whether there were any problems with people being
abused in your household when we first interviewed
you.  (PAUSE) When you compare then and now, would you say things
are now   READ RESPONSES

( ) 1 Much better
2 Somewhat better
3 About the same
4 Somewhat worse
5 Much worse
6 No problems then or now

| ECONOMIC SELF-SUPPORT AND SECURITY--CLIENT ABOUT SELF |
|---|

( , , , )_ _ _ _Client I.D.

( ) 1 Intake

2 Follow-up

( ) ① Questionnaire Version

( , ) ⑪ Module Number

---

INTERVIEWER:  IF CLIENT IS IN INSTITUTION, GO TO Q. 122

The next few questions ask about your economic situation.  They will take only a few more minutes of your time.

116.  In the past month, have you or other people in the household had trouble paying bills?  Would you say there were  READ RESPONSES

( ) 1 No problems
2 Minor problems
3 Medium problems
4 Major problems

---

117.  In the past month, have you had enough money for food, clothing, fuel, shelter and transportation for the people in your household?  Did you go without things you needed?  Would you say there were  READ RESPONSES

( ) 1 No problems
2 Minor problems
3 Medium problems
4 Major problems

---

118.  Are you currently in debt?  If so, is it  READ RESPONSES

( ) 1 No problem
2 Minor problem
3 Medium problem
4 Major problem

---

119.  During the past month, Were you  READ RESPONSES

( ) 1 Employed full-time  SKIP TO Q. 120

2 Employed part of the time  ASK b

3 Unemployed, looking for work  SKIP TO Q. 122

4 Unemployed, not looking for work  ASK a

a.  What is the main reason you were not looking for work?

( , ) 11 In school or training
12 Retired
13 Preferred to stay home taking care of house and/or children
14 Sick or disabled
25 Believed no work was available, lacked necessary skills, or had given up
26 Could not arrange child care, care of invalid
_7 Other reason (specify)

SKIP TO Q122

| COORDINATOR:   CODE LEFT DIGIT FOR LAST RESPONSE |
| 1=AGENCY DOES NOT TRY TO REMOVE PROBLEM |
| 2=AGENCY DOES TRY TO REMOVE PROBLEM |

b.  What is the main reason you were not working all of the time?

( ) 11 In school or training
12 Retired
13 Preferred to stay home taking care of house and/or children
14 Sick or disabled
25 Could not find full-time work, or had given up looking
26 Could not arrange child care, care of invalid
_7 Other reason (specify) _____

| COORDINATOR:   CODE LEFT DIGIT FOR LAST RESPONSE |
| 1=AGENCY DOES NOT TRY TO REMOVE PROBLEM |
| 2=AGENCY DOES TRY TO REMOVE PROBLEM |

---

ECONOMIC SELF-SUPPORT AND SECURITY--CLIENT ABOUT SELF, CONT'D

---

120. How would you rate your satisfaction with your current job?  Are you  
READ RESPONSES

( ) 1 Very satisfied  
2 Somewhat satisfied  
3 No feelings one way or the other  
4 Somewhat dissatisfied  
5 Very dissatisfied

---

121. On your current job, how many hours per week do you work?  How much are you paid?

_____ Hours per week

$ _____ per _____

TRY TO OBTAIN GROSS PAY.  IF RESPONDENT KNOWS ONLY TAKE HOME PAY, MARK "TAKE HOME PAY" ON QUESTIONNAIRE

MONTHLY PAY WILL BE CALCULATED AND CODED BY COORDINATOR

( ) 1 $700 or more per month  
2 $500 to $699 per month  
3 $400 to $499 per month  
4 $300 to $399 per month  
5 $200 to $299 per month  
6 $100 to $199 per month  
7 Less than $100 per month

---

122. In the past month, did you and the other members of your immediate household receive income from any of the following public assistance sources?

a. From Welfare--AFDC or general assistance?

How much all together for everyone?

( ) 1 No  
2 Yes ASK HOW MUCH  
( , , )_ _ _Amount in past month to the nearest dollar

b. From Supplemental Security Income (SSI) (a gold check)?

How much?

( ) 1 No  
2 Yes ASK HOW MUCH  
( , , )_ _ _Amount in past month to the nearest dollar

c. Food stamps?

How much?

( ) 1 No  
2 Yes ASK HOW MUCH  
( , , )_ _ _Amount in past month to the nearest dollar

---

ECONOMIC SELF-SUPPORT AND SECURITY--CLIENT ABOUT SELF

---

READ THIS QUESTION SLOWLY AND CAREFULLY.  FOR CLIENTS IN INSTITUTIONS ASK ONLY
ABOUT THEIR OWN INCOME, NOT EVERYONE "IN HOUSEHOLD."

123.  Now I would like to know about how much income your household/  ( , , , )_ _ _ _Income to the nearest dollar
you had last month, not counting any money you got from welfare
or supplemental security income (a gold check).  Please think
about how much money everyone in the household received.  Think
about money from jobs, from social security (a green check),
from disability, from railroad retirement, from unemployment, from
pensions, from child support or alimony, or workmen's compensation,
from providing foster care or day care, or from any other non-welfare
source.  About how much money all together came into your household
last month?

IF CLIENT HAS DIFFICULTY WITH THIS QUESTION, PROBE BY ASKING ABOUT EACH
DIFFERENT KIND OF INCOME INDIVIDUALLY.  AN EXACT FIGURE IS NOT NECESSARY,
BUT SHOULD BE AS CLOSE AS POSSIBLE.  IDEALLY WITHIN $10 OR SO.

---

COORDINATOR:  ADD TOTALS OF Q. 122 AND 123 AND USE POVERTY TABLES
WITH HOUSEHOLD SIZE TO FIND RELATION TO POVERTY LINE

Total of Q. 122 and 123 _____

( ) 1 Over 125% of poverty line
2 Poverty line to 125%
3 75% to poverty line
4 Below 75% of poverty line

ASK ONLY AT FOLLOW-UP

124.  Now think about whether you had money problems when we first interviewed
you.  (PAUSE)  When you compare then and now, would you say things are
now  | READ RESPONSES |

( ) 1 Much better
2 Somewhat better
3 About the same
4 Somewhat worse
5 Much worse
6 No problems then or now

125.  Is there any problem you would like to mention which we have not
talked about?  Problems with family, health, feelings--or anything
else?
_____
_____
_____

---

That is all the questions.  Thank you very much for your patience and helpfulness.

## OUTCOME INFORMATION OBTAINABLE FROM GOVERNMENT RECORDS

As indicated in Exhibit 1, case records or other agency records can be sources of information on certain client outcomes. Below are listed examples of such information.

Physical Health

R-1 Client has died

------------------------------------------------------------------------------------

Mental Distress

R-2 Client attempted or committed suicide since intake
R-3 Evidence of at least one incident of a nervous breakdown since intake

------------------------------------------------------------------------------------

Alcohol and Drug Abuse

R-4 Evidence of at least one arrest or conviction related to use of alcohol during past three months
R-5 Evidence of at least one arrest or conviction related to use of drugs during past three months

------------------------------------------------------------------------------------

Child Welfare

R-6 Frequency and severity of recurrence of abuse or neglect
--No indication of child abuse or neglect
--Reported but unconfirmed case of child abuse or neglect
--Confirmed case of child abuse or neglect
--Child removed from home temporarily due to recurrence of abuse or neglect
--Child removed from home permanently due to recurrence of abuse or neglect
--Injury to child resulting from abuse
--Death of child as result of abuse

R-7 Time taken for placement (by type of placement)
--Child placed within, for example, ninety days after decision to seek placement
--For "hard to place" child: child placed within, for example, six months after decision to seek placement

R-8 Placement status[a]
--Improvement: Institution to own home
Foster home to own home
Institution to adoption
Foster home to adoption
Institution to foster home
--No change: Continuing in own home
Continuing in foster home
Continuing in institution
Continuing in adoption
--Deterioration: Changed foster home; foster parents unable to continue care
Changed foster home; incompatible foster home
Went from foster home to institution
Child transferred to another institution for reasons other than age or improvement in conditions
Child placed in institution within twelve months of being discharged from another institution (recidivism)

a. The validity of this hierarchy depends on the changes in placement being appropriate. Other information, such as on client functioning, should be used along with the data on placement status.

# APPENDIX 2.

## RATIONALE FOR THE ILLUSTRATIVE

## OUTCOME QUESTIONNAIRE

# APPENDIX 2

## RATIONALE FOR THE ILLUSTRATIVE OUTCOME QUESTIONNAIRE

Chapter 2 discusses the general principles underlying the client outcome questionnaire; Appendix 1 contains a version of that questionnaire. This appendix discusses the rationale underlying the choice of questions and question wording and the sources from which questions were adapted. Our initial report contains additional discussion of the questionnaire's content and derivation.[1]

The questionnaire presented in Appendix 1 is the version which is used to interview an adult or adolescent client about the client's own condition. There are two other versions--one for an adult being interviewed about a child client and one for an adult being interviewed about an adult client who for some reason cannot be interviewed. These two "alternate" versions are, of course, cast in the third person, and there are some modifications in questions in some modules, which are noted in the discussion of each module in this appendix.

The modular structure of the questionnaire permits an agency to add questions in areas of special interest (or to delete questions that are less important to that agency). For example, Durham County added the following questions to the Background Information module:

-- where the client had sought other help before coming to the social service agency

-- who had referred the client to the agency

-- whether having to wait for an appointment was a problem for the client

-- whether the client understood why the agency had to work with the family (for Protective Service clients only)

A number of people were being referred inappropriately to the Department of Social Services, and the Department officials hoped by means of the first two questions to identify some of the sources of referrals. The third question related to concern about the agency intake system, by which nonemergency clients had to wait several days for an appointment with an intake worker. The fourth question reflected the agency's concern with client understanding of the reason for protective services investigations.

---

1. Annie Millar, Harry Hatry, and Margo Koss, Monitoring the Outcomes of Social Services, vol. 1 (Washington, D.C.: The Urban Institute, 1977).

More detailed outcome information might be needed by an agency on any of the client functioning areas, or on areas not covered in the illustrative questionnaire. Questions or modules can be added.

If questions are added, the agency should be careful to test the new questions for understandability and lack of bias. In adding questions, an agency should always consider how much they will lengthen the interview and how much additional time is required to analyze the resulting data.

Following is a rationale for each module of the client outcome questionnaire. Appendices 3 and 4 present other pilot test findings on the reliability and validity of the questionnaire.


## Module 1.  Background Information

The questions in this module contain basic information about the client-- age, sex, race, household composition, marital status, and level of education-- that can be used to break out outcome data by different client groups. The entire module is administered in the pre-service interview. At the follow up some of the background questions could be dropped, but we suggest that at least the questions on age and sex be retained as a doublecheck that the respondent is the correct person. Household composition and marital status also should be asked at follow up, since they may change after intake.

In addition to demographic information, this module includes the question, "What problem or problems led you to come for help at the Social Services Department; what kind of help do you want?" Clients in the pretests in Chesapeake and in Stanly County gave vague or incomplete answers to this question on "presenting problems," while caseworkers who were asked to describe their clients' presenting problems usually listed more and different problems. However, it seems worthwhile to obtain clients' perceptions of why they have come, and to compare these perceptions to subsequent outcomes of services. (Case record information on presenting problem, if it exists and can easily be collected, might be gathered to supplement client responses.) This question also provides an introduction to the rest of the questionnaire.

Two different ways of asking the "presenting problem" question were used in the pilot tests. In the Chesapeake pretest, interviewers read a list of problems to clients and asked them to say which problems they had. Interviewers found this list difficult and time-consuming, so it was dropped from the main pilot tests. Asking the introductory question in an open-ended fashion means that someone (probably the coordinator) has to code the responses. Although this is more work for the coordinator, it will keep the interview more efficient.

In the two "alternate" versions, the questions in this module are asked in the third person--about the client--and the relationship of the respondent to the client is asked.


## Module 2.  Client Satisfaction

The questions in this module, administered only at follow up, ask clients about their satisfaction with the specific services they received and with some aspects of their treatment by agency staff. Clients are also asked whether their overall condition has improved and whether they think the services they received have had helpful or harmful effects on their problems.[1]

In answering questions about their satisfaction with services, clients in the pilot tests had difficulty differentiating between social services and public assistance programs such as food stamps, medicaid, and financial assistance. (Agencies could, of course, also ask about satisfaction with financial assistance, but this might be more appropriately handled in a separate study.)  Interviewers need to be well trained to assist respondents in making this distinction. Also, clients often do not realize that they have received services such as "counseling" and "information and referral" because they are not concrete services or services that clients had specifically asked for.  This posed a problem in asking about satisfaction with such nonconcrete services.  In the Chesapeake follow up, clients were asked to name the services they received and rate their satisfaction with each of these.  Comparison of client responses with information from records regarding services received showed that clients sometimes omitted or misnamed services, in addition to confusing financial assistance with services.  Therefore, we now recommend that clients be read a list of the services that the records show they received.  Since data on services are to be collected from records anyway, for analysis, this does not mean more work for the coordinator; it only means that the service data must be collected before the follow-up interview.  The interviewers may have to explain to clients what some of the service terminology means, but this approach appears to be the only way to assure that data on satisfaction are obtained on all services for which the agency is accountable for each client.

Besides services provided directly by the social services agency, clients may be referred to other agencies or may obtain other community services on their own.  Since these other services may also affect outcomes, it seems desirable to find out what other community services clients received.  Agencies might want to go one step further, as did Chesapeake, and add questions regarding clients' satisfaction with referrals and with subsequent services from outside agencies to which they had been referred by the social services bureau.

There are a number of specific aspects of service quality that could be included in the satisfaction questions--whether clients felt workers understood them, whether the agency's location and hours were convenient, and so on.  Our choice of questions on specific aspects was guided by the general principle that they should concern things an agency might be able to modify.  Agencies will undoubtedly differ in their choices of questions in this area, depending on their specific concerns.  There are many satisfaction questionnaires in use around the country, and agencies could substitute a set of questions from one of these or add their own questions.

---

1.  In the pilot tests, the questions in the Client Satisfaction module were supplemented by questions (at the end of each problem module) that asked whether they thought the specific problem area had improved and which services, if any, had had good or bad effects on that problem area.  Interviewers and clients found the latter questions tedious and repetitive, and clients had considerable difficulty in attributing good or bad effects to services.  Because of these difficulties, we deleted the questions from the illustrative questionnaire.  The questions asking for client perceptions of whether specific problems have improved are retained.  They are not as difficult to ask, and they provide another perspective (the client's opinion) to add to the change calculated from the before and after interviews.

Most questions ask clients to give details if they are "dissatisfied" with services. These open-ended responses have to be hand-tabulated.

This module also includes two questions on the number of contacts with case-workers. These questions are included here for convenience; they are not related to "satisfaction" per se, but are used to augment information on services obtained from records for correlation with outcomes. If reliable information on number of contacts is available from agency records, these questions could be deleted from the client questionnaire.

## Module 3. Physical Health

One approach to measuring "health" would be to ask about specific medical disorders, physical handicaps, medications, and so on, but we were unable to find an instrument of reasonable length that elicited such information and aggregated it into a meaningful estimate of overall health status. More importantly, it appears that social service agencies are more concerned with the effects of health problems on functioning and well-being than with the exact nature of the health problems. Therefore this module consists of a question about clients' perceptions of their overall health and two questions regarding the extent to which health problems interfere with clients' functioning. One question is related to the "restricted-activity days" concept used in the Health Interview Survey of the National Center for Health Statistics, and the other is a slightly more subjective "perception" question. (Responses to these two questions appear highly correlated, and one might be dropped.) The Activities of Daily Living module, which follows the Physical Health module, elicits more detailed information regarding functional limitations and the help clients receive with activities of daily living.

In the pilot tests, questions regarding the outcomes of family planning services were added, but their formulation posed some problems. Use of family planning is an "intermediate" outcome. The "ultimate" outcome is the prevention of unwanted pregnancy, and this is difficult to measure. The concept of "unwanted pregnancy" is problematical, and it is not a frequent event, so that within a nine-month time frame for an outcome study, the absence of an "unwanted pregnancy" may not be a particularly informative outcome. Also, if an "unwanted pregnancy" had occurred shortly before intake, another would be less likely in the next few months regardless of the success of family planning. An agency, however, might still choose to look at the intermediate outcome of use of birth control, or to gather information on incidence of unwanted pregnancy among clients. Clients did not show any reluctance to answer these questions, although we do not have any information regarding the accuracy of their responses.

Another "intermediate" outcome question included by the jurisdictions has been retained in the illustrative questionnaire because it seems of interest to most public social service agencies—whether clients had problems obtaining medical care. In our tentative socring procedure, however, the responses to this question are not scored together with the pure "outcome" questions in the module, but are retained as a separate category of "explanatory" information that is relevant to specific policy on health-related services. The principle under which we omitted it from the general score was that if improved access to medical care resulted in improved health, this would show up in the other questions. If an agency felt that the intermediate outcome of improved access to medical care was an outcome of primary importance, however, the agency might choose to include such an outcome in the overall health score.

As noted in the discussion of the satisfaction module, each of the problem area modules has a question for follow up regarding clients' perceptions of how their problems in that area have changed since the pre-service interview. Thus, at the end of the Physical Health module, there is a question regarding the clients' perceptions of whether physical health changed.

## Module 4. Performance of Activities of Daily Living

Day-to-day self-care activities can be divided into (1) "chore" or "domestic" activities such as shopping, cooking, and housework, and (2) personal care activities such as bathing and dressing. Social services agencies provide assistance with both types of activities to severely disabled persons and assistance with "chore" activities to somewhat less disabled persons who can handle personal care but cannot perform the more demanding domestic tasks. There has been considerable measurement work in this relatively concrete area of functioning, and several questionnaires have been developed by others. Among those which we reviewed before constructing this module were the Lawton-Brody Instrumental Activities of Daily Living scale, the Duke University OARS scale, the Katz Activities of Daily Living Index, the Barthel Index, and the HEW Patient Classification for Long-Term Care.[1] These instruments provide somewhat more detail than we wished to include as part of an outcome monitoring instrument covering several areas of functioning, so we selected a few questions that were common to most of the scales and which our advisors and test jurisdictions considered important for an outcome assessment--shopping, cooking, housework, and laundry among the "chore" activities; bathing, eating, toileting, and taking medicine among the personal activities; and mobility both inside the home and in traveling outside of the home.

Initially, we focused solely on the issue of clients' own capacity to perform these activities and the extent of the help they needed. The outcome to be assessed was improvement or deterioration in clients' self-care capacities and in the levels of help they required. During the course of the field tests, however, our orientation has changed somewhat. Social service agencies are also concerned with whether the chores and personal care activities are adequately performed by the homemakers or chore workers, or whoever does them, as well as with any rehabilitative effects on clients. Particularly for chronically ill and elderly clients, the maintenance of decent conditions and the slowing of deterioration are important goals of services regardless of whether any "improvement" in self care can be expected. Therefore we modified the questions, so that they now ask not only about clients' capacity to perform these activities themselves, but also whether they are satisfied with the way

---

1. M. Powell Lawton and Elaine M. Brody, "Assessment of Older People: Self-Maintaining and Instrumental Activities of Daily Living," The Gerontologist 9, no. 3 (Autumn 1969): 179-86; Duke University Center for the Study of Aging and Human Development, Older Americans Resources and Services Program, "OARS Multidimensional Functional Assessment Questionnaire" (Durham, N.C., April 1975); Sidney Katz et al., "Studies of Illnesses in the Aged, The Index of ADL: A Standardized Measure of Biological and Psychosocial Function," Journal of the American Medical Association 185, no. 12 (September 21, 1963): 914-19; Florence I. Mahoney and Dorothea W. Barthel, "Functional Evaluation: The Barthel Index," Maryland State Medical Journal, February 1965; U.S. Department of Health, Education, and Welfare, Patient Classification for Long-Term Care: User's Manual, by Ellen W. Jones (Washington, D.C.: DHEW pub. no. HRA74-3107, December 1973).

in which the activities are performed (possibly by a combination of their own efforts and any help they have).  Questions as to whether clients are helped (and who helps) are also included to assist an agency to determine the relation of the type of help received to client satisfaction with how the activities are performed.  This new question format has not been tested in any of the jurisdictions, but the test agencies believe it is a sound approach.

Since many social service clients are not physically disabled, and asking this series of questions of nonimpaired clients is unnecessary, tedious, and possibly annoying to clients, we decided after the pretest in Chesapeake to include "screening" questions.  Before proceeding with the detailed "chore" questions, the interviewer asks whether the client has difficulty with any of these types of activities, and a similar general question is asked before the detailed "personal" activities questions.  During the course of the pilot pre-service interviews in Chesapeake, however, we found that disabled clients who couldn't do chores but had help with chore activities were answering the chore screening question as "no problem," and thus skipping the detailed questions.  In order to avoid this misinterpretation, the screening question for "chore" activities problems was revised so that clients who would have difficulty, regardless of whether they have help, will be asked the detailed questions that follow.  Interviewers should be well trained to avoid "screening" out impaired clients whose chores are performed by others.  Interviewers also should be trained to help clients separate physical problems involved in shopping, say, from money problems that cause them to be unable to buy the things they need.

In the alternate version for an adult being interviewed about a child age thirteen or younger, the "chore" activities questions are not asked, since these activities are the responsibility of adult caretakers.  The entire module is skipped for children under age five.


## Module 5.  Mental Distress

Modified versions of the first ten questions from the Denver Community Mental Health Questionnaire[1] have been used for measuring mental distress.  This short and easily administered set of questions attempts to assess symptoms that contribute to "mental distress."  It is important to note that these ten questions (questions 38-47 in Appendix 1) are not intended to be scored and displayed individually.  One score is to be calculated for the set of ten questions.  Any individual can, on occasion, display a few of the individual

---

1.   James A. Ciarlo and Jacqueline Reihman, "The Denver Community Mental Health Questionnaire:  Development of a Multi-Dimensional Program Evaluation Instrument" (Denver, Colo.:  Mental Health Systems Evaluation Project of the Northwest Denver Mental Health Center and the University of Denver, 1974).  This questionnaire has been used primarily to measure the functioning level of different samples of clients at successive time intervals; it has not yet been used to compare "before and after" readings on the same clients or even the same group of clients.  Nonetheless, there appears to be no reason why it cannot be used to assess "change" scores for the same clients.

symptoms. The discriminating ability of the scale derives from collective consideration of the responses to all ten questions.[1]

The Denver questions ask the client about the last couple of days. For
the purposes of outcome assessment, in order to avoid transient symptoms, the
time reference has been changed to ask about the month immediately preceding
the interview. In addition, the words "indigestion" and "fatigue" in the Denver
questionnaire were changed to "upset stomach" and "feeling very tired," since
the North Carolina pretest showed the former terms to be more difficult for
respondents to understand. Some clients in the Chesapeake pretest had difficulty with the phrase "tense or uptight"; Stanly and Durham counties preferred
to substitute "nervous or worried." These changes could affect the validity
of the scale, although we have no evidence that this is so. In the first
phase of our work, the ten-item scale, using the past month as the time refer-
ent, was used in a statewide citizen survey conducted by the state of Wisconsin
covering approximately one thousand randomly selected households. It appears
that the scale differentiates between nonclient and client populations. For the
Wisconsin general population sample, less than 10 percent of the respondents had
scores higher than eleven (the range of scores is zero to thirty, with higher
scores representing worse symptoms), and approximately 50 percent had scores of
five or below. Scores on the same scale in the Chesapeake pre-service interviews included a much higher percentage of scores above eleven (37 percent) and
a larger percentage with scores of five or below (32 percent). In addition,
the percentage of "high" scores at follow up was lower than pre-service, indicating some capacity to identify change.

Because the DCMHQ has been administered to nonclient populations in Wisconsin and elsewhere, that data can be used to provide "community norms" with
which to compare client scores—both pre- and post-treatment scores. Such comparisons will enable public officials to assess how close to the general population's distress levels, client mental distress levels are.

There are other mental health scales available, but the brevity of the
Denver scale, in the absence of evidence that other, longer scales provide substantially superior data, appears to leave the shorter scale with an advantage
over these others.[2]

---

1. The Denver team has conducted several tests of the validity and reliability of the original scale. These indicate its ability to discriminate between clients of mental health programs and the general population. The Denver
team compared (1) scores obtained from clients with those based on interviewer
judgments (the correlation coefficient was 0.94 for a sample size of 349);
(2) scores obtained from clients with ratings made by persons who knew the
clients well (the correlation coefficient was 0.59 for N=91); (3) client scores
with global ratings made by clinicians (the correlation coefficient was 0.35
for N=71); and (4) client scores with scores obtained from a sample of Denver
residents (the Denver scale was found to differentiate between the two sets of
respondents). See also David C. Speer, "An Evaluation of the Denver Community
Mental Health Questionnaire as a Measure of Outpatient Treatment Effectiveness"
(Columbus, Ind.: Quinco Consulting Center, 1976).

2. The Symptom-90 Checklist is easy to understand and administer and deals
with a wider variety of distress symptoms, but contains ninety items. Leonard
R. Derogatis, Ronald S. Lipman, and Lino Covi, "SCL-90: An Outpatient Psychiatric Rating Scale—Preliminary Report," Psychopharmacology Bulletin 9 (1973):
13-28; and Leonard R. Derogatis, et al., "The Hopkins Symptom Checklist (HSCL):
(Footnote 2 continued on following page.)

In addition to the ten-item modified Denver scale, this module includes a question on loneliness and one on suicidal feelings. The "loneliness" question was added because of concern with social isolation, a target of certain social services such as socialization groups, senior citizens centers, and counseling. Some of the instruments we reviewed included questions regarding the actual amount of social contact achieved by clients, such as questions on the frequency of telephone conversations. Without some accepted norm or criterion for determining "adequate" levels of contact, however, such "objective" information is difficult to interpret. We preferred to obtain clients' subjective judgments of loneliness rather than impose our own judgments as to how much contact represents "isolation" or lack of it.

The question on suicidal feelings was included to supplement the Denver questions, as a possible additional symptom of severe depression. If this question is found highly correlated with scores on the ten-item scale, it might be deleted or, alternatively, serve as a reliability check.

In the alternate version of the questionnaire for adults being interviewed about children, this module is omitted for children under five and modified for children between five and thirteen to delete less appropriate questions such as those on suicidal feelings and to add questions on nightmares and bedwetting. The "adult about another adult" version includes all the questions, but respondents frequently don't know about clients' feelings, and so this module appears likely to have low reliability in this third-person version.

## Module 6.  Family Strength

The questions in this module ask about several types of family problems that clients might have. There are many specific problems in marital relationships, parent-child relationships, and other areas of family life that could conceivably be included. In the interest of brevity, we tried to select a few questions that would encompass these various specific problems; other agencies might wish to include more detailed questions in this module. The

---

A Self-Report Symptom Inventory," Behavioral Science 19, No. 1 (January 1974): 1-15.

The questionnaire used in the midtown Manhattan study, with twenty-two items, has been administered to the general community to estimate the incidence of mental health problems. T. S. Langner, "A Twenty-Two Item Screening Score of Psychiatric Symptoms Indicating Impairment," Journal of Health and Human Behavior 3 (1962): 269-76; and L. Strole et al., Mental Health in the Metropolis: The Midtown Manhattan Study, vol. 1 (New York: McGraw-Hill, 1962). One study, however, found that an abbreviated set of nine items in this questionnaire provided results similar to those obtained by using all twenty-two items. Jerome G. Manis et al., "Validating a Mental Health Scale," American Sociological Review 28, no. 1 (February 1963): 108-16.

Another instrument in this area is the Health Opinion Survey. See Dorothea C. Leighton et al., The Character of Danger: Psychiatric Symptoms in Selected Communities (New York: Basic Books 1963); Allister M. Macmillan, "The Health Opinion Survey: Technique for Estimating Prevalence of Psychoneurotic and Related Types of Disorder in Communities," Psychological Reports 3, supp. 7 (1957).

approach chosen is similar to that of the Family Services Association of America's (FSAA) follow-up questionnaire.[1] The FSAA questions elicit clients' perceptions of the improvement in several family problem areas. Two of our questions are modifications of questions on the FSAA questionnaire--"handling arguments and working out differences" and "feeling close."

In addition to questions regarding relationships among family members within the clients' households, there is a question regarding problems in relationships with family and close friends outside of the household. For clients living in substitute care, there are questions regarding contact with their own families, and institutionalized clients are asked about relationships with other clients or staff within the institution.

Comparison of clients' self-report scores on this module with their caseworkers' ratings showed that caseworkers frequently perceived more serious problems than clients reported. Further testing is indicated to discover if there is a problem with these questions or a serious underreporting bias in the client responses.


## Module 7. Quality of Substitute Care

For clients in foster homes, group residences, or institutions, this module elicits information on their satisfaction with the quality of care provided. (Interviewers are informed before the interview about whether clients are in substitute care.) Clients' satisfaction with such care is not the only possible measure of the quality of care; "trained observer" inspection of conditions would provide different and in some ways more objective data. Clients' perceptions, however, are important in themselves and should probably be a part of any assessment of the quality of substitute care arrangements. This set of questions represents the consensus of the test jurisdictions regarding appropriate items of interest; it is by no means the only possible set of questions.

In the alternate versions, if the client lives in the home of the person being interviewed, the module is skipped, as it does not seem appropriate to ask the "caretaker" about the client's satisfaction with the caretaking.


## Module 8. Child Behavior and Parenting

The instruments currently available for assessing child behavior are lengthy and are generally linked to specific age groups and certain categories of problems. For outcome monitoring purposes it is impractical to use different instruments for different categories of children, and so a few basic and readily observable types of behavior problems were selected by ourselves and

---

1. Dorothy Fahs Beck and Mary Ann Jones, How to Conduct a Client Follow-Up Study (New York: Family Service Association of America, 1974); and Beck and Jones, Progress on Family Problems: A Nationwide Study of Clients' and Counselors' Views on Family Agency Services (New York: Family Service Association of America, 1973). Further discussions of the findings are presented in articles in Social Casework: Beck and Jones, "A New Look at Clientele and Services of Family Agencies" (December 1974); Beck, "Research Findings on the Outcomes of Marital Counseling" (March 1975). See volume 2 of the first-phase report for details.

the test jurisdictions from among the questions included in other instruments.[1] As with the other modules, agencies may wish to alter the choice of questions to fit their interests.

Certain questions are inapplicable to some ages of children; skip patterns are used to avoid asking inapplicable questions. For example, the question regarding running away, "keeping bad company," and breaking curfews is asked only in regard to adolescents. For adolescents being interviewed about themselves, questions regarding the adolescents' own perceptions of their problems are substituted for the set of questions "about" the children in the household that are asked of adults with children. The only question "about" other children that is asked of adolescents is the single question about very young children that is asked of adolescent respondents who are parents.

The format of the "child problem behavior" questions has undergone considerable change in the course of the pretests and pilot tests. Originally, each question would be asked about each child in the household; this led to long interviews for clients with several children. We thus decided to ask for a collective judgment of the severity of each problem among all the children. In the pilot tests for "major" and "medium" problems, the respondents were asked to give the number of children that had the problem. However, we found that these extra questions on number of children added little information; few clients listed more than one child per problem, and in the few cases where more than one child had problems, the problems were very severe regardless of the number of children or else the number of children with problems did not change much from pre-service to follow up. Therefore we dropped these questions for the illustrative questionnaire shown in Appendix 1.

In addition to asking about each child, the original questionnaire also contained more detailed questions than most other modules. Since the questionnaire's purpose is primarily measurement of outcomes for many clients rather than diagnostic assessment of individual clients, such detail is unnecessary. Therefore, subsequent to the pilot tests, we reviewed the pilot test data and talked with the pilot test working group in Chesapeake, seeking ways to shorten this module. Separate questions that concerned related behavior or received highly correlated responses have been combined as shown in

---

1. The instruments upon which we drew included the Devereux Adolescent Behavior Rating Scale, The Devereux Child Behavior Rating Scale, and the Devereux Elementary School Behavior Rating Scale; these are fully discussed in Oscar Krisen Buros, ed., The Seventh Mental Measurements Yearbook, vol. 1 (Highland Park, N.J.: Gryphon Press, 1972), pp. 67-68. We also drew upon the Washington Symptom Checklist, a 76-item inventory of child behavior gleaned from complaints of parents seeking help in a child psychiatry clinic. Herbert C. Wimberger and Robert J. Gregory, "A Behavior Checklist for Use in Child Psychiatry Clinics," Journal of the American Academy of Child Psychiatry 7 (1968): 677-88. We examined the Child Behavior Characteristics Schedule, a 104-item checklist of "bad" and "good" behaviors. Patricia W. Cautley and Martha J. Aldridge, Predictors of Success in Foster Care (Madison, Wisconsin: Wisconsin Department of Health and Social Services, 1973), pp. 255-56. The National Institute of Mental Health's Handbook of Psychiatric Rating Scales, 2nd ed. (1973), identifies other scales for rating child behavior and symptoms.

Appendix 1. (For example, breaking curfews, keeping bad company, and running away have been combined into one question; five detailed questions on school problems have been combined into one.)

Another measurement issue which was debated in this module, as well as in some others, was the questions of "anchored" versus "unanchored" response categories and "frequency" versus "severity" response categories. In this module, we originally asked for the frequency with which a problem occurred in the past month--once, two to five times, six to ten times, eleven or more times. One of the pilot test agencies also considered anchoring the "major," "moderate," and "minor" categories to specific frequencies. We eventually decided not to use frequencies because we had no basis for interpreting the significance of different frequencies. As in the issue of "isolation" in the Mental Distress module, it seemed better to obtain the clients' judgments of severity rather than try to impose our own. Frequency would not, in any case, capture the severity and importance of any single episode or series of episodes. One "lie" might be important if it injured someone else, and ten "lies" might be unimportant if they were the normal "fantasy" stories that many children tell.

This entire module is deleted in the "adult about another adult" version because most cases will not involve clients who are responsible for the care of children.

Module 9.  Alcohol and Drug Abuse

Social services clients may be reluctant to divulge socially and legally unacceptable behaviors. In some cases, such as Protective Services cases where the agency is considering removal of children from the home, clients may have compelling reasons to deny drug or alcohol abuse. Because of concern with this issue in the pilot test, this module used more than one approach to assessing abuse; questions asking about both quantity of consumption and consequences were included, plus a set of questions designed to detect "hidden" alcoholism.

There are some instruments that have been tested by others and show some ability to discriminate between alcoholics and nonalcoholics, and we drew upon these tested questions. The four questions of the "CAGE" instrument are included as question 97 in the section of the module that deals with alcohol abuse.[1] These four questions were developed in an attempt to identify "hidden alcoholics." Three positive replies to these questions indicate a strong possibility of alcoholism, and even two indicate some possibility. When the responses of patients in an alcoholism rehabilitation center were compared with those of a set of nonalcoholics, the instrument differentiated between the two groups. Respondents did not object to answering these questions.

-----

1.  J. Ewing and B. Rouse, "Identifying the 'Hidden Alcoholic,'" paper presented at the 29th International Congress on Alcohol and Drug Dependence, Sydney, Australia, February 2-6, 1970, p. 3. The acronym CAGE refers to the content of the four questions: "Cut down," "Annoyed," "Guilty," and "Eye-opener." See also Demmie Mayfield, Gail McLeod, and Patricia Hall, "The CAGE Questionnaire: Validation of a New Alcoholism Screening Instrument," American Journal of Psychiatry 131, no. 10 (October 1974): 1121-23.

Although the CAGE questions appear to be a means of identifying alcoholics, they were not developed as a way to assess <u>changes</u> in alcoholism. They should be able to reflect a change from alcoholic to nonalcoholic, but may not be sensitive to changes of lesser magnitude.

The Denver Community Mental Health Questionnaire includes a set of questions on alcohol and drug abuse and the negative consequences of such abuse. We drew upon their questions in formulating questions about the extent of drug use and about whether drinking or drug use had caused problems with job or school, with friends or family, and so on.

Although the pilot test findings on this module are limited because relatively few clients had drinking problems, and almost none had drug problems, there is evidence that the questions on alcohol consumption and the CAGE questions are more sensitive and obtain more information than the other questions on problems resulting from drinking. There were thirty-nine interviews in which clients reported either heavy consumption (five or more drinks in a day) or any drinking problem. Heavy drinking was reported in twenty-six interviews and "yes" answers to one or more of the CAGE questions in twenty-four interviews, but other problems and "having a drinking problem" were reported in only nine and three interviews respectively. In the nine interviews in which problems resulting from drinking were reported, seven clients also answered "yes" to one or more CAGE questions, as did two of the three clients who admitted to having a drinking problem. If further testing confirms this finding that the "problem" questions add relatively little information, they might be eliminated or collapsed into one general question such as, "In the past month, have you had any problems resulting from your drinking, such as problems at work, with friends or family, accidents or fights, or trouble with the law?" A similar condensation of the drug questions might also be indicated, but there were not enough pilot test data to explore this possibility, since very few clients had drug problems.

Honesty of responses is an even greater concern in the drug abuse questions, since the nonprescription use of these drugs is illegal. Obtaining this information from such sources as police records or relatives would be difficult, if not inappropriate (invasion of privacy), but an agency might consider reviewing case records on this issue to at least check how often clients who are known to their caseworkers as having substance abuse problems deny them in these interviews.

A screening question was included for the alcohol section to avoid asking clients who have not drunk in some months about recent problems with drinking.

Some additional questions were included regarding adolescent drinking problems, since indicators of adult alcoholism are not always applicable to adolescent problem drinking.

Although prescribed drugs may be abused, we found in the field tests that asking about prescription drugs as well as nonprescription drugs caused interviewing problems. Many clients take prescription drugs and most do not abuse them; asking all of the abuse questions of clients taking blood pressure medication, or other drugs for medical reasons, proved awkward and annoying to some clients. The "loss" involved in missing a few cases of abuse of prescription drugs seems a small price to pay for avoiding these problems.

In the alternate version for adults being interviewed about children below the age of adolescence, this module is deleted entirely.

## Module 10. Physical Abuse

This module's questions ask about abuse of the client and of other members of the household. Whether or not medical care was required is used as a rough indicator of the severity of any episodes of abuse. The question set includes a query about the relationship of the abuser to the client. This provides some additional descriptive detail to the agency and also permits separation of abuse within families from incidents of assault involving strangers. Although the latter type of abuse may sometimes be an issue in adult protective services, social service agencies are more often concerned with abuse within families or social networks.

Since client frankness is a concern in this area, it is recommended that record data be collected on this issue to supplement client reports. In the pilot tests, no clients whose records or caseworkers reported abuse failed to report it in the interview, but a few clients reported abuse that was not mentioned by the record or caseworker. The number of cases in the pilot test with abuse problems was so small, however, that these data do not provide dependable evidence regarding the reliability of these questions.

## Module 11. Economic Self-Support and Security

Social service agencies provide services to help clients maintain or improve their standard of living (to at least acceptable minimum levels). Services are concerned with educating and training clients and helping them find jobs; helping them seek and obtain various monies to which they are entitled, such as child support or welfare benefits; and helping them manage better with whatever money they have. This module includes questions related to each of these aspects: changes in amount of income; changes in how well the income is managed to meet household needs; changes in employment status and the quality of employment; and changes in the degree of dependence on welfare.

The employment questions address whether or not clients have jobs full or part time, their job satisfaction and earnings, and reasons for not working or working less than full time. Other instruments commonly include scales to assess "employability" of respondents. Considering this an "intermediate" outcome, we chose to focus instead on the "ultimate" outcome of whether or not the client was working. However, agencies might choose to include an employability scale, and, in fact, a measure of employability of clients at intake might be useful for classifying clients by "difficulty" in order to better interpret the outcome findings.

The income questions caused some difficulty. Initially, we sought household income by asking about each possible type of income--Social Security, earnings, private pensions, and so on. The long series of questions was tedious for interviewers, and clients were sometimes confused and sometimes reluctant to give such detailed answers. After the pilot test intakes and the Chesapeake follow up made it clear that the information obtained was costly in terms of effort and of questionable accuracy in any case, it was decided to ask simply for the total household income from nonwelfare sources, and assistance from each of the main welfare sources--AFDC and general assistance, Supplemental Security Income (SSI), and food stamps. The outcome "indicators" derived from these income data are the relation of total household income to the federal (and state) poverty lines, the change in level of dependence upon welfare assistance, employment status, and the extent to which the income is meeting household needs.

# APPENDIX 3.

## PILOT TEST EVIDENCE

## REGARDING THE QUESTIONNAIRE'S VALIDITY

APPENDIX 3

PILOT TEST EVIDENCE REGARDING THE QUESTIONNAIRE'S VALIDITY

Appendix 2 provided the rationale for the questions included in the Client-Outcome questionnaire presented in Appendix 1. That rationale presented some of the findings from our pretests with clients of the questionnaire wording. This appendix summarizes the findings of a number of other tests we undertook relating to the questionnaire's validity and reliability. These tests led to some additions, deletions, and modification of questions in the questionnaire, and some refinement in the scoring procedure. The following paragraphs describe our efforts.

1. Case Record Review (Chesapeake). Chesapeake and Urban Institute personnel examined fifty case records from various service divisions. We wanted to determine whether the problems and goals discussed in the records were covered in the questionnaire. The problems and outcomes in these cases were generally quite well-covered in the questionnaire. Family Planning was the only outcome area that was not covered (Chesapeake elected to add a Family Planning question). Some wording improvements were suggested by the findings, and a screening question was added to enable nondisabled clients to skip the Activities of Daily Living questions. Overall, this review indicated the appropriateness of the questionnaire's content.

2. Caseworker Interviews and Case Record Checks (Chesapeake and Stanly County). When the questionnaire was pretested, the reliability of client responses was checked in three ways. (1) Twenty-five clients interviewed in the pretest of the questionnaires were reinterviewed three to four days later, and their answers from the two interviews were compared. (2) The caseworkers of twenty-six pretest clients (largely clients whose cases had been open for some time) were interviewed using the same questionnaire; they were asked to assess the clients' problems. Their responses were compared to the clients' responses. (3) Factual data in the case records of forty-two pretest clients were compared to factual data in the interviews--such as age, family composition, income, employment.
Except for a few questions that gave clients and interviewers difficulty (which were subsequently either deleted or modified), the questionnaire appeared to elicit reliable responses. The clients' responses in the initial interviews substantially agreed with their responses on reinterview, with the caseworkers' assessments, and with the factual data in the case records. (The factual data available in records sometimes did not include income, employment, and household composition information.)
In addition, these tests were consistent with the hypothesis that caseworkers would be unable to report on some areas of client problems and well

being, particularly those concerning clients' feelings and problems that were outside the focus of casework.

3. <u>Caseworker Judgments of Severity of Clients' Problems</u> (Chesapeake). We developed a tentative procedure for "scoring" the individual questions to obtain summary scores for each problem area and for problems overall. Seven professional social workers (five from Chesapeake and two from The Urban Institute) and one lay person (one of The Urban Institute staff), who had not seen the tentative scoring procedure, read six questionnaires that had been completed by clients and rated the severity of the clients' problems. Then we compared the "mechanical" scoring procedure to the "personal judgments" made. The "mechanical" scoring matched well with the "personal judgment" procedures.

4. <u>Caseworker Retrospective Ratings</u> (Chesapeake). The caseworkers of eighty-five of the Chesapeake clients who had been interviewed in the pilot test (both pre-service and follow up) were asked to give ratings of severity of the clients' problems in each problem area. They were asked to rate how severe the clients' problems were at intake and at the time of the caseworker interview nearest to the time of the pilot test follow-up client interview. These caseworker responses were compared to the client responses.

Caseworkers' and clients' reports were similar in over three-quarters (77 percent) of the ratings (see Exhibit A3-1). When they differed, client reports most frequently indicated more serious problems than caseworker reports indicated. Although it is possible that clients were overestimating their problems, it seems more likely that they had problems about which they had not told their caseworkers. This appears especially likely in the area of Child Problem Behavior, where a third of the clients reported significant problems that the caseworkers did not report. In one area, Family Strength, this pattern was reversed, however. This may indicate a problem in the Family Strength questions, it may indicate that clients underreport family problems, or it may indicate that caseworkers are more concerned about family conflict than are clients. These possibilities should be explored further when the questionnaire is used again. The significant finding here is that while there were some instances where a client denied a problem that the caseworker knew about, there were many more cases (about 2-1/2 times more) in which the caseworker was not aware (probably had not been told by the client) of a significant problem.

5. <u>Statistical Reliability Checks of Questionnaire</u> (Durham). North Carolina's Department of Human Resources conducted a series of statistical tests covering responses from forty-one clients of the Durham test. The findings of this limited examination indicated that internal reliability of the questionnaire was generally good. Appendix 4 details these findings.

Overall, the questionnaire appears to provide data with reasonably good validity and reliability. As noted in Chapter 2, with respect to "face validity," the questionnaire represents a consensus among a number of social workers and administrators as to the important possible outcomes of social services. This consensus held up with only minor differences among the agencies involved in the pilot tests. The review of case records in Chesapeake, noted above, confirmed the appropriateness of the questionnaire's content.

EXHIBIT A3-1.  COMPARISON OF CASEWORKER RATINGS
OF THEIR CLIENTS' PROBLEM SEVERITY
WITH THE CLIENTS' SELF-REPORT SCORES[a]

| Problem Area[b] and Time | | Percentage of Cases in Which Caseworkers' Ratings... | | |
|---|---|---|---|---|
| | | Were Similar to Client Self Report[c] | Indicated More Serious Problem than Client Self Report[d] | Indicated Less Serious Problem than Client Self Report[d] |
| Physical Health | – Intake | 70% | 6% | 24% |
| | – Follow up | 69 | 8 | 23 |
| Mental Distress | – Intake | 68 | 8 | 24 |
| | – Follow up | 72 | 8 | 20 |
| Family Strength | – Intake | 68 | 22 | 10 |
| | – Follow up | 76 | 12 | 12 |
| Child Problem Behavior | – Intake | 61 | 4 | 35 |
| | – Follow up | 62 | 0 | 38 |
| Alcohol/Drug Abuse | – Intake | 94[e] | 1 | 5 |
| | – Follow up | 92[e] | 0 | 8 |
| Physical Abuse | – Intake | 99[e] | 0 | 1 |
| | – Follow up | 99[e] | 0 | 1 |
| All areas, both intake and follow up | | 78% | 6% | 16% |

---

a.  The caseworkers of eighty-five clients in the Chesapeake pilot test provided retrospective ratings of their clients' problems at intake and at the time of the casework contact nearest in time to the pilot test follow up.

b.  Two problem areas are excluded.  Activities of Daily Living was not defined on the caseworker rating form, and a number of caseworkers did not understand that this referred to problems in doing chores or self care due to disability or illness.  Economic Security and Self Support was omitted because it was not clear which of several subscores (Poverty, Dependence on Welfare, Employment, Money Management) should be compared with a single caseworker rating.

c.  "Similar" means that the caseworkers' rating differed by no more than one letter on the following scale:  A (no problem), B (minor problem), C (medium problem), and D (major problem).

d.  "More Serious" and "Less Serious" indicate a difference of more than one letter.

e.  These percentages are so high because nearly all clients and caseworkers reported "no problem" in these areas.  However, there were almost no instances where a client denied a problem that the caseworker knew about, but there were several cases in which the caseworker was not aware (probably had not been told by the client) of a significant problem in these serious areas.

# APPENDIX 4.

## RELIABILITY OF SELECTED ITEMS

## USED IN THE CLIENT QUESTIONNAIRE

RELIABILITY OF SELECTED ITEMS USED IN THE

CLIENT QUESTIONNAIRE*


The meaningfulness of findings obtained from this instrument depends upon the reliability and validity of the questions or items used to measure client status (functioning or condition).

Reliability refers to whether a measure is consistent; validity addresses whether an item measures what it is supposed to measure.

We will address two aspects of reliability. "Equivalence" refers to a person's position (response) on different questions intended to measure the same thing. "Homogeneity" refers to the consistency of a person's responses on a number of items or questions measuring the same subject domain.

The tests for reliability reported herein are based on a subset of the persons interviewed in this study. Only responses of clients who answered the interview questions themselves and for whom there is both an intake (pre) and a follow-up (post) interview have been utilized. A total of forty-one clients met these two conditions. To have included other interviews (for example, an "other" about client) would introduce additional sources of potential unreliability, making it difficult to focus on the reliability of the questions themselves.

Table A4-1 summarizes the findings regarding internal reliability (consistency). For each pair of measures, several statistics are reported. A measure of association (either Cramer's V or the Contingency Coefficient, C) is reported which describes the degree of association between the responses to the paired questions. For some questions, Kendall's tau (ordinal data) or Pearson's rho (interval data) are used to describe the degree of association. These statistics generally range from 0 (no association) to ±1 (a perfect "one-to-one" association).[1] A third statistic, lambda, is also a measure of association. It is based upon the concept of "proportional reduction in error" and may be interpreted as the percentage improvement in prediction of responses to one question when the responses to another question are known [in comparison to making a guess based upon the category with the most cases (the mode)]. Values for Lambda range from 0 (no improvement in prediction) to 1.0 (prediction can be made without error). In addition, for the mental health scale (Ciarlo), Cronbach's alpha is used to assess internal consistency. In Table A4-1 the question used to predict responses on another question is listed

---

*This analysis was prepared by Lee Kittredge, Chief, Evaluation Section, Department of Human Resources, state of North Carolina. It is based only on North Carolina (Durham) data.

1. The contingency coefficient, C, does not attain the maximum upper limit of one.

first. Thus, for example, the two questions--reason not working or only working part time and reason not looking for work--were answered similarly. The
association is fairly strong (C=.876), and there is a 60 percent improvement
(over predicting from the mode) in predicting responses to the second question
when the answers to the first question are known. These statistics indicate
that the reliability (in this case "equivalence" as a form of consistency) is
good for the two questions.

With two exceptions, the items analyzed appear to have good reliability--
that is, the responses to different questions measuring the "same thing" or the
same subject domain are consistent. Exceptions are items which required the
client to rate his/her own change in physical health and mental health at follow
up compared to that at intake. When the client's own rating is compared to a
more objective change score (based upon the difference between pre and post
responses), the associations are weak in both cases. This suggests that a
client's self report which requires recall of health status changes over time
(in this case, nine months) is probably an unreliable indicator of actual
change.[1]

---

1. This difference was expected; it has generally been found in other
studies comparing client perceptions of improvement to information obtained
from more "objective" measurement procedures. This difference is a principal
reason why client perception of change is considered a separate and different
outcome dimension. This is also a major reason why procedures that only use
client perception of improvement to measure client outcomes (thereby avoiding
the need to use pre-service interviews of clients) do not appear adequate.

Table A4-1:  Internal Reliability

| Items or Variables | Number of Cases | Test Statistic(s) | Significance Level[1] | Reliability |
|---|---|---|---|---|
| Reason not working, or only part time, past three months<br>with<br>reason not looking for work (intake version) | 14 | C=.876<br>lambda=.600 | .006 | "Equivalence" is good |
| Reason not working full time (intake)<br>with<br>reason not working, or only part time, past three months | 13 | C=.862<br>lambda=.669 | .009 | "Equivalence" is good |
| Days incapacitated due to illness (intake)<br>with<br>rating of physical health | 41 | C=.575<br>tau=.449<br>lambda=.207 | .016<br>.001 | "Homogeneity" is fairly good |
| same items follow up | 40 | C=.656<br>tau=.548<br>lambda=.185 | .0004<br>.001 | "Homogeneity" is good |
| Extent health problems interfere with desired activities (intake)<br>with<br>rating of physical health | 41 | C=.597<br>tau=.549<br>lambda=.276 | .007<br>.001 | "Homogeneity" is good |
| Same items follow up | 41 | C=.641<br>tau=.612<br>lambda=.222 | .0008<br>.001 | "Homogeneity" is good |
| Marital status asked twice at follow up* | 39 | V=1.00<br>lambda=.960 | .000 | "Equivalence" is excellent |

Table A4-1 (continued)

| Items or Variables | Number of Cases | Test Statistic(s) | Significance Level[1] | Reliability |
|---|---|---|---|---|
| Ciarlo 10-Item Mental Health Scale# | | | | |
| at intake | 40 | alpha=.797 | | "Homogeneity"-good |
| at follow up | 39 | alpha=.933 | | "Homogeneity"-good |
| Respondent's own rating of change in physical health pre-post with pre-post physical health rating change score | 41 | V=.359 tau=.202 | .385 .061 | "Equivalence" is weak |
| Respondent's own rating of mental health change pre-post with mental health change score | 36 | rho=.344 tau=.274 | .02 .018 | "Equivalence" is weak |

[1]Significance level for C or V statistics is based on chi-square test.

*One discrepancy (error) probably due to interviewer coding judgment.

#Ciarlo reported an alpha of .85 in developing this scale. See Ciarlo and Reihman, "The Denver Community Mental Health Questionnaire: Development of a Multidimensional Program Evaluation Instrument," in Coursey et al., Program Evaluation for Mental Health (Grune and Stratton, 1977).

Symbols:

      C=Contingency coefficient
      V=Cramer's V
      lambda=Lambda asymmetric
      tau=Kendall's tau correlation coefficient
      rho=Pearson's correlation coefficient
      alpha=Cronbach's coefficient alpha

Note: The SPSS package was used to calculate these statistics. Nie et al., Statistical Package for the Social Sciences, second edition (McGraw-Hill Company, 1975).

Table A4-2 reports data on internal consistency which bears upon construct or convergent validity--the association of nonidentical items which theoretically ought to be associated (measure the same characteristic).  In this case, a person's mental health status as measured by the Ciarlo scale should be associated with feelings about suicide.  One would expect that those with "good" mental health would be less likely to report feelings of suicide than those with "poor" mental health.  The measure of association (V) and the lambda coefficients indicate that this is indeed the case, especially for clients at time of follow up.

Table A4-2:  Consistency of Mental Health Scale Responses and Responses to Suicide Questions (Convergent Validity)

| Items | Test Statistics | Significance Series |
|---|---|---|
| Ciarlo Scale with Suicide-intake: | V=.828 lambda=.5000 | $\alpha$=.046 |
| Ciarlo Scale with Suicide-follow up: | V=.897 lambda=.75 | $\alpha$=.009 |